All profits from the sales of this ~~~~~~~~~ ~~ ~~~~ ~~ support of
Christian Outreach opportunities to the Mormon People and
activities that Promote and Protect the First Amendment of

The Constitution of the United States of America

For additional information on the History, Beliefs, Practices and
Doctrines of The Mormon Church

Read:

Mormonism – A Life Under False Pretenses

The
True Story
of a
Mormon Bishop's Journey of Discovery

By Lee B. Baker

Jailed for Teaching
The Gospel of Jesus Christ in America

The True Story of Mormon Corruption in Indiana

By Lee B. Baker

Former Mormon High Priest and Ordained Bishop

Explanation of Narrative Style and a Legal Notice from the Author:

What follows is the true story of six days within the violent Marion County Jail, Indianapolis, Indiana, among brutal Federal, State and County Inmates from a wide-ranging degree of criminal backgrounds and convictions. In 2014, the "Indy Channel," RTV-6 (*ABC* Affiliate) reported 20 deaths within the Marion County **Jail**, six times the rate per capita as the Indiana State **Prison**. As a suspected Felon, my entire time was spent among some of the most violent and wicked of men from the Midwest. I will accurately and truthfully document the interactions and conversations of my incarceration with one practical restriction. Please note that I have elected to substitute the overwhelmingly profane and sexually-graphic language with selected replacement expressions. Given the subject matter and the character of the participants, I am confident that the reader will deeply appreciate these replacement expressions when needed. This graphic and true story has been developed and issued under an Ex Parte Order for Protection from the Marion County, Indiana, Superior Court, Criminal Division, Case Number 49G21-1507-PO-024527, and as such this information is for **You** (the reader) and is **Not** intended (directly or indirectly) for the Petitioners (aka: Mr. Paul H. Sinclair or Indianapolis Deputy Chief of Police, Bryan K. Roach). The following information and my comments are **About** Mr. Sinclair, Partner of the Law Offices of Ice Miller and a Senior Leader within the Mormon Church, and **About** the Indianapolis Deputy Chief of Police, Mr. Bryan K. Roach and is **not** **To** Mr. Sinclair, the Law Firm of Ice Miller or any of their Clients or **To** the Indianapolis Deputy Chief of Police, Mr. Bryan K. Roach. As such you are instructed **Not** to share this information **With** Mr. Sinclair, the Law Firm of Ice Miller or any of their Clients or **With** the Deputy Chief of Police, Mr. Bryan K. Roach. If you do distribute, communicate or cause this information to be distributed or communicated with Mr. Sinclair, the Law Firm of Ice Miller or any of their Clients or Mr. Roach, either directly or indirectly, you may be at risk of legal action. The information, observations and comments within this short story are exclusively the personal opinions of Mr. Lee B. Baker. The information, observations and comments within this short story are for informational purposes only and are **NOT** intended or designed as any form of harassment, intimidation, defamation or stalking. *What follows is intended as a **Public Notice** of **One Man's Opinion**.* As an active member of the Press Corps, the International Radio Media, a Christian Minister and a Retired Disabled Veteran of the United States Military, I request your support in promoting and supporting our collective **Freedom of Speech**. This literary work is published under the protection and authority of the United States Press Agency – Reporter of Religion: Mr. Lee B. Baker, UPA Media Group ID Number: I-US/VI-01/31941, Las Vegas, Nevada. United State of America

"Any Free American Christian who will stand for Nothing... will fall for Anything."

Introduction

For those American readers who may still not fully comprehend the current attacks on your Personal Freedoms and Civil Liberties, Please sit down and buckle-up. At our home in California on the morning of Wednesday, the 2nd of March 2016, I received a completely outrageous and excessively oppressive Plea Agreement[1] from the State of Indiana. To both demonstrate and confirm what I believe to be the unethical and corrupt connection among the State of Indiana, the Law Firm of Ice Miller, and the Mormon Church, I have included an original copy of that first Plea Agreement as Appendix C. The Plea Agreement from the State offered to dismiss All remaining charges, if I would agree to Never Discuss this Story[2], to Never Report this Story, to Never to Publish this Story, to Never to Comment on this Story, to Never be Interviewed about this Story and to Never Contact the Mormon Church on <u>any subject</u> in any manner, means, method or mode for a period of three years.

For 36 consecutive years I served the United States of America with distinction, dedication and courage. For that entire time I held a Top Secret security clearance with Special Access to the Nation's most sensitive Intelligence information within The National Security Agency and the Central Intelligence Agency. This unethical offer from the State of Indiana was absolutely and completely unacceptable on several levels.

---

[1] See Appendix C: Plea Agreement – State of Indiana v. Lee Baker
[2] With any of the millions and millions of Americans associated with any of the over 500 clients of Ice Miller, LLP.

This abuse of power and the clearly unethical influence between Indianapolis City Officers and a secret Mormon Priesthood allegiance is intolerable. The political corruption documented here extends well beyond any professional courtesy or acceptable level of influence between the Police, the Courts and a Senior Mormon Leader.

At the very foundation of basic human rights, our Public Officials, Officers and trusted members of the Community, simply should not treat its Citizens this way. I have presented the Gospel of Jesus Christ to hundreds in Indiana and I have accurately contrasted the vast differences between Mormonism and Christianity. And I have responsibly completed both assignments without a single lie and without any deception. As a result, I am now a convicted criminal beginning a very restrictive three-year probation. I have been officially and legally advised to watch carefully **what** I say and **who** I say it to.

Therefore, at the real risk of 3 to 5 years within one of the many brutal Indiana State Prisons, here without compromise or embellishment, is my graphic but True Story of Mormon corruption in Indiana.

Preface

It would not be for several weeks after I was thrown across the cell, over the steel table and onto my back, that I would learn the black teardrop prison tattoo just below his right eye was the mark of a murderer. What I did recognize for certain, was that with an erratic arterial condition, already exhausted and just a few months shy of age 60, the beating promised that evening from this 6' 3" inch, thirty-something hoodlum would not go well. Not well at all.

As I picked myself up, hung my head and began to return to my bunk I heard: "*Hey, Old School, you jack-ass, come back here and clean-up your mess!*" My violent and unscheduled launch over my lunch had scattered the remainder of the marginally edible food across the floor of the "Gladiator Pit" on the 4th floor of the Marion County Jail in downtown Indianapolis. I slowly bent down and began to pick up the few scattered peas and carrots, as the cornbread and milk had been taken from me earlier. There, on my hands and knees, with a chorus of very graphic profanities in the background, I wondered how... how did I come to be here?

Just two days earlier I was prepared and smugly confident that I could and would not only represent myself well in Court, but I might even take the opportunity to preach a bit to my accuser and even to the Judge if necessary. The brutal fact was my hearing started at 1:30 in the afternoon of September 23rd, 2015, and by 1:45 I was shackled in chains. True humility is often acquired very swiftly and most often at an exceptionally unreasonable price. On that, the second day of six behind bars with murderers, rapists and thieves, I stood as a supreme example of precisely that expensive education.

What follows is the short story of precisely how an articulate, if somewhat arrogant, College Educated, 36-year Veteran of the National Security Agency and Grandfather of ten, with no criminal record, found himself in a large urine and blood stained communal cell with 38 other suspected or convicted Felons. As the only elderly white male and certainly the only inmate without a tattoo, the distrustful looks and finally the piercing questions began within the first hour. "*So...what's your deal Old School?*" and "*Are You a Cho-Mo or what?*"

Without my "*Papers,*" the slang for a copy of my formal Court charges, the exceptionally unlikely story that I had been arrested only for sending religious emails did not sound accurate, much less would that alone have earned me a bunk on the 4th floor with the worst of the worst. I then mistakenly added the fact that I

4

had been charged with 3 felonies and 18 misdemeanors. Although it was true, this additional information only confirmed their suspicions. *"Screw you, Cho-Mo,"* they said and walked away disgusted. To be accepted by the welcoming committee of the "Gladiator Pit" would never have been an anticipated highlight of my life, but now, to be thoroughly rejected by them was terrifying. With the established assumption that I was a child molester (*Cho-Mo*) among 38 Federal, State and County Felons, suddenly the impact of the lies told about me rapidly accelerated from just offensive and vengeful to potentially lethal.

Background

This true story of corruption within the Mormon Church and the City of Indianapolis, documents the dishonesty, collusion and vengeful actions of The Indianapolis Metropolitan Police Department and the Law Firm of Ice Miller, LLP[3]. Additionally, what will be presented here is a clear demonstration of one man's immature and reckless misuse of the Legal System for personal gain. More importantly, from a theological perspective, this narrative clearly demonstrates the enormous chasm between Christianity and Mormonism.

It was both the depth and breadth of that immense chasm between Christianity and Mormonism that drove one of the most senior leaders of The Mormon Church in the United States of America to an astonishing display of irrational and absurd professional behavior. Generally speaking, irrational and absurd professional behavior, when restricted to the workplace, is extremely common and often mildly entertaining. The truly disturbing nature of *this* professional outburst is rooted in my opinion, that within *his* profession, he egoistically exercised the full power of the Police, the Laws and the Courts of the State of Indiana. Mr. Paul H. Sinclair, a

---

[3] See Appendix A: Listing of the major clients of the Law Firm of Ice Miller, LLP.

Partner within the Law Firm of Ice Miller, LLP, and a very senior Mormon "Elder," most often called a "General Authority," could not bring himself to discuss even the simple and basic Doctrines of Mormonism. So, frustrated and without any alternative or ability within himself, I believe he turned to the Courts out of professional embarrassment.

You are probably wondering how did all of this get started and how did it then get so blown out of proportion? As a former High Priest and Ordained Bishop within the Mormon Church, I was invited, along with my wife Kathy, to join a well-organized three-week Christian Outreach opportunity just north of Indianapolis. The unique occasion was a Temple Open House sponsored by the Mormon Church to commemorate the completion of their 148th Temple. Within the upscale hamlet of Carmel, Indiana, the Mormon Church has erected a stunning building worth an estimated $52 million dollars that will be used by only a very, very small percentage of the Mormon people.

The three-fold purpose of this Christian Outreach was to bring the Gospel of Jesus Christ to the local Mormon Community, educate the local Christian Community specific to the fundamental beliefs and doctrine of the Mormon Church, and to provide an authoritative and reliable face-to-face resource for Mormon religious questions and debate issues. The latter is imperative due to my experience and consideration that the members of the Mormon faith are both intentionally and thoroughly ignorant specific to the true history and doctrine of their own Church. This deliberate barrier of knowledge allows the average Mormon to maintain a selective awareness of some non-Christian practices, while stressing the more commendable social and service elements of their faith.

Nearly one hundred thousand, newspaper-style 12-page "Non-Mormon Temple Visitor's Guides[4]" were widely distributed to the local community in support of this exceptionally focused religious educational opportunity. This guide provided examples of little known but certainly authorized teachings and doctrines of the Mormon faith, including the belief that God was once a man and that all men (like Mr. Paul H. Sinclair) can become Gods.

Additionally, as recorded within the current publication of the Book of Mormon[5], the Doctrine[6] that a skin of "Blackness" was God's curse upon the wicked and faithless men and women on this earth is found. It is a current Mormon Doctrine that White skin indicates righteousness and purity and that Black skin indicates rebellion and wickedness. Much to the irritation of the local Mormon leadership, the Indianapolis area media recorded a graphic demonstration of one of the lesser-known but truly repulsive elements of Mormon history. This "in the flesh" exhibition highlighted the fact that Joseph Smith Jr., the founder of Mormonism, had nearly 40 secret wives, many of them the current wives of other men.

In the hot afternoon sun of Saturday the 25th of July 2015, 34 young girls and women from several area Christian Churches volunteered to dawn pioneer style dresses and reverently stand in a silent line depicting only a fraction of the wives of Joseph Smith, founder of the Mormon faith. Each of these women was familiar with the personal history of the wife they represented and were able to recount to the visitors and media the horrific conditions of Mormon polygamy. The vast majority of Mormon visitors ridiculed this demonstration and incorrectly reassured themselves that it was all just a lie. The fact was (according to official Mormon documents[7] that Joseph Smith, at the age of 37, had between 30 and 40 wives

---

4 http://ancestryworship.com/AncestryWorship/LDS_TOPICS/LDS_TOPICS.html
[5] Book of Mormon, 2Nephi, Chapter 5, Verse 21 with 3Nephi, Chapter 2, Verses 14-16 and 3Nephi, Chapter 19, Verses 25,30 or Mormon, Chapter 5, Verse 15
[6] See Appendix D: Racist Doctrine from the 2016 version of the Book of Mormon
[7] https://www.lds.org/topics/plural-marriage-in-kirtland-and-nauvoo?lang=eng

and several were just 14 years old. Most visitors were appalled to learn from official Mormon records that over a dozen of Joseph's additional "secret" wives were the wives of other living Mormon men, who essentially just shared[8] their wives, a night at a time, with Joseph.

During the three weeks we answered questions and produced copies of the authorized Mormon doctrine, manuals, teachings and policies. We also accurately recounted for the visitors the specific ceremonies, rituals and secret handshakes to be accomplished within all Mormon Temples. During my time in Carmel, I worked closely with the well-dressed senior Mormon Security Representative, a Mr. Bryan K. Roach. Brother Roach was a local High Priest in the Mormon Church who was asked, by Mr. Paul H. Sinclair, to lead a 14-member Church Committee responsible for security, parking and traffic flow during the Temple Open House.   A well-spoken and agreeable man, Brother Roach was very responsive to both the local Police Department and our group of Christian volunteers, referred to by the Mormons as the "Protesters."

Within the all important Mormon hierarchy of Priesthood authority, Mr. Paul H. Sinclair, an Indianapolis attorney, holds the very senior position of a Mormon Area Authority, formally addressed as, "Elder Sinclair." This very high-ranking position within the Mormon Church is considered the ultimate authority, as he reports directly to the Apostles of the Mormon Church in Salt Lake City, Utah.   Elder Sinclair is without question the senior representative of the Mormon Church, not only in Indiana but across the entire Midwestern United States of America. The functional religious rank difference between Brother Roach and Elder Sinclair is equivalent to an ordinary Army tank Sergeant and a highly esteemed Three-star Lieutenant General.

---

[8] https://www.lds.org/topics/plural-marriage-in-kirtland-and-nauvoo?lang=eng

In working on a daily basis with Brother Roach, he would routinely communicate to me the several directions and decisions of Elder Sinclair. Elder Paul H. Sinclair, in the Mormon world, was then and is now the most senior and direct representative of the Mormon God's only living Prophet. He is considered by the Mormons as the only man on earth who is authorized to speak and act for the God of Abraham, Isaac and Jacob. His authority, position and respect are not only to be continually revered; it is actually considered a major violation of the Mormon Temple Endowment to even question Elder Paul H. Sinclair. To do so as a Mormon is an act of defiance and insubordination worthy of excommunication.

With a printed invitation and ticket in hand, on the afternoon of Friday, the 17th of July, my wife Kathy and I entered the southeast door of the Mormon Temple along with the twelve other visitors in our small group. Once deep within the hallways and meeting rooms of the Temple, I noticed a tall distinguished looking man with a formal nametag, gold embossed, proclaiming the title "Elder Sinclair." I stepped towards him with an extended hand and whispered "Elder Sinclair, Good Afternoon." At the conclusion of our one-hour tour, I was interviewed at our information tent by Maverick Atteberry, a videographer at Indianapolis FOX-59 and CBS-4, who then interviewed Elder Sinclair near the main doors of the Mormon Temple.

After a short discussion with two Mormon Sister Missionaries, I again met Elder Sinclair on the grounds of the Temple and I asked if he would consider answering three basic questions[9] about the Mormon Church. He asked where I was from and who I was. After I answered these questions, he instructed me to wait on the steps of the Temple for his return as he had a prior appointment to attend to. He said, *"I'll be right back."* I waited 45 minutes in the rain, but he never returned.

---

[9] See Appendix E: Three Basic Questions for Elder Sinclair

The next day I returned to the Mormon visitor's tent and inquired about Elder Sinclair. I asked if I could get a message to him concerning his request that I should have waited for him the previous day. After several diversionary conversations with more Sister Missionaries, it became obvious that Elder Sinclair had no intentions of meeting with me. I returned to the Christian visitor tent and resumed answering questions about the Mormon Church.

On that next Monday, the delightful and well-dressed Brother Roach again visited our tent and asked if there were any security or procedural issues to discuss. I told him of my short meeting with Elder Sinclair, to which he stated *"Yes, I saw you talking with him."*

Not to belabor the point, but it is my opinion that Elder Sinclair lied to me. Not only did he lie to me, but I believe he lied in Court under Oath. As part of my cross-examination of him, on the 23rd of September, I asked Elder Sinclair if we had ever met before. He stated twice, *"No"* and *"Never."* I reminded him, in Court and under Oath, that we spoke about an interview there at the Mormon Temple. Again he said, *"No."*

Yet in his written Affidavit, again under Oath, and recorded in his own Law Office taken by Detective Matthew A. Morgan on the 2nd of September, Elder Sinclair on the first page of his legal statement admits that he told Mr. Baker, *"That's not gonna happen"* and he walked away without any *"further interaction"* with Mr. Baker.

At this point I would offer some friendly advice to the reader in an attempt to alleviate any confusion you might have. Please consider what you and I may have come to know as the dangers of either perjury or deception in the Court, will have a very flexible definition here, given that the City of Indianapolis is represented by the Law Firm of Ice Miller, who is the employer of Elder Sinclair.

It should also be noted, although I did not know it at the time, the Officer (Detective Matthew A. Morgan) taking the Affidavit from Elder Sinclair works for the Deputy Chief of the Indianapolis Metropolitan Police Department. That Deputy Chief is a Mormon High Priest by the name of Bryan K. Roach, who serves the Mormon Church at the request of Mr. Paul H. Sinclair, who in turn serves the City of Indianapolis who is in turn represented by the Law Firm of Ice Miller LLP., who in turn employs "Elder" Paul H. Sinclair. It felt like I was in south Chicago in the 1930's.

From that point on, if I saw Elder Sinclair walking around the Temple grounds, I shouted and yelled to him from the public sidewalk for some of his valuable time. Rightly so, he found this embarrassing, offensive and rude, but it was certainly not illegal.

Even as a former Mormon Bishop and member of that faith for over three decades, I was absolutely astonished by the far-reaching power and control of the secret Mormon Priesthood into the non-Mormon world there in Indiana. On Friday, July 31, I was approached by two Deputies of the Hamilton County Sheriff's Office (Officer Chris Yates and Officer Jason Cramer), who served me with a formal one-page "Ex Parte Order for Protection."

Beyond all reason and rationality, Elder Paul H. Sinclair, himself an Attorney of some reputation, persuaded the Marion County Superior Court that I was in fact a legitimate and legal threat of violence to him and his family. As such I was formally served with an order to cease any harassment or the annoying (with Religious or Any Other issues) of this Mormon Official; this 6' 4", 235 lbs, former BYU Football player who had lied to me.

As a well-coordinated bonus, within the sealed Official Packet of Court Orders from Myla A. Aldridge, Clerk of the Marion Circuit Court, Criminal Division, were two threatening letters, one from The Law Firm of Ice Miller and the other from The Church of

11

Jesus Christ of Latter-day Saints, Salt Lake City, Utah. Each letter informed me that I was no longer welcome on their respective properties and strongly suggested that I should correct my behavior or additional legal action would be taken.

I was immediately puzzled: how, when and why had the Tax Payers of Indiana, the Marion County Superior Court and the Deputies of the Hamilton County Sheriff's Office become a free, yet fully armed courier service for Elder Sinclair's Law Firm of Ice Miller and the vindictive Headquarters of the Mormon Church over 1,500 miles away?

Given the generally accepted level of Church and Government corruption usually associated with the "Beehive" State, it would appear that a corrupt slice of Utah had now come to Indiana. To further clarify, within an Indiana Church building owned by the Mormon Faith a formally stamped and sealed packet of Court documents was opened at the direction of a Mormon Deputy Chief of Police, to add two non-Court documents from a Mormon Attorney's Firm and the Headquarters of the Mormon Church all without the knowledge or authorization of the Marion County Superior Court.

I did not completely comprehend the sinister and threatening ramifications of this unauthorized tampering with Official Court documents, until I became fully aware of the non-Mormon, public responsibilities of Brother Bryan K. Roach, the ever faithful minion and subordinate of the high-ranking Mormon Elder, Paul H. Sinclair. With discovery that the Indianapolis Metropolitan Deputy Chief of Police himself had been using his influence and authority to manage some exclusively Mormon issues, a disturbing event at the beginning of our visit to Indiana suddenly became clear.

During the first week of Outreach to the Mormons, which was supported by several local Indiana Christian Churches, I was handed a copy of a threatening email from an angry local Mormon. I personally delivered a copy of this email to both Sergeant John McAllister of the Carmel Police Department and Mr. Bryan Roach, before I knew he was the Deputy Chief of Police. The threatening email specifically implied physical harm to the Christians who participated in the Outreach to the Mormons and ended with several profanities. Mr. Roach did not seem at all concerned about the aggressive email. He told me, "*Lee...Don't worry about it.*" In the weeks to come he did <u>not</u> provide any explanation or follow-up information. In hindsight, it is very strange indeed how my truly non-threatening emails questioning the integrity of Mr. Sinclair became a Felony Offense and yet a clear threat of physical harm to local Christians did not deserve even a second-look. Mr. Roach and Mr. Sinclair sure seemed to be a very proficient team of Mormon High Priests, when properly motivated.

A week or so after departing Indiana, I received several very peculiar phone calls from Christian law enforcement Officers whom I had never met. Each Officer, from three different western States, informed me that the State of Indiana had just issued a Nationwide Police Intelligence Report. This sensitive report was issued by the Indianapolis Metropolitan Police Department stating that a "Mr. Lee Baker" (two photos were provided) had threatened to "*kill a Mormon Elder on Temple grounds*" and should be approached with caution.

Knowing my current Mission work and my past history with the Mormon Church, these considerate Officers contacted me first as a warning and second for some clarification as to the reported statement. One Utah State Patrol Officer met me at an Interstate roadside rest area and showed me the actual report. I found it very interesting that no Indiana Investigator, Detective, Police Officer, Court Officer, Probation Officer or Mall Cop has ever asked <u>me</u> about the reported statement or of the intended "murder." Yet this completely invented reference can be found within Mr. Paul H.

13

Sinclair's formal charges, statements and the affidavit for probable cause.

Some clarity is gained when one learns that the source of the alleged statement from Mr. Baker provided to the Indianapolis Police was the Headquarters of the Mormon Church in Salt Lake City. More clarity is gained when one learns that the untrue and fictional police report against Mr. Baker was issued by the Deputy Chief of the Indianapolis Metropolitan Police Department. Still more clarity is gained when one learns that the Deputy Chief of Police is Brother Bryan K. Roach, who serves the Mormon Church at the request of Mr. Paul H. Sinclair, the influential attorney from Indianapolis. And clarity about the act of coercion and intimidation is further enhanced when one learns that it was Deputy Chief of Police, Officer Bryan K. Roach, who personally placed the additional letters from his Church and his Church Supervisor's Law Firm into the sealed Official Court Packet from the Honorable Judge Patrick Dietrick.

These events, as reported by the Sheriff[10] of Hamilton County, establish both the reasonable impression and the demonstrated reality that an immoral and dishonest link exists among the Leadership of the Indianapolis Metropolitan Police Department, the Leadership of the Law Firm of Ice Miller, the Leadership of The Mormon Church and the Prosecutor, Clerk and Officers of the Marion Superior Court, who willfully failed to corroborate the claims of Mr. Paul H. Sinclair because of his unethical and close association with the Deputy Chief of Police.

I am convinced that due to Mr. Sinclair's weak character and obvious embarrassment, moreover his apparent religious frustrations, the only practical option left was for him to use the Courts as his personal instrument of retribution. What is so extraordinary to me is

---

[10] See Appendix B: Emails To and From the Hamilton County Sheriff

14

that he will not, and perhaps cannot, rationally express himself face-to-face concerning his connection to the racist and sexually motivated Doctrines found within the Mormon Church.

I frankly admit that it was my ignorance and overconfidence that caused me to violate the Court Order, and yet, I do feel that I was skillfully and deliberately baited into a position of *"Contempt of Court."* Without thinking, I did respond to the officially delivered Contempt of Court hearing issued by The Clerk of the Marion Circuit Court, filed with Court 21 of the Criminal Division, signed by a Marion Superior Court Judge, certified by State of Indiana and yet very strangely emailed to me by... yes, Mr. Paul H. Sinclair, the very person with whom I was ordered <u>not</u> to have any contact. No doubt this event was a source of entertainment among the attorneys at Ice Miller, who each knew that such a *"No Contact"* restriction is valid **only** for the *"Respondent,"* me, and need not be respected by the *"Petitioner"* Mr. Sinclair. Yes, I am sure that around the offices of Ice Miller, it was hilarious for a week or more; even I considered it well played.

So... this is why I was arrested; this is why I was put in Jail as a suspected Felon among murders, rapist and thieves — because I responded to Mr. Paul H. Sinclair with these eight simple words: *"Outstanding, I will see you in two weeks."* Had I truly threatened violence towards anyone or had I simply been an embarrassment to Mr. Sinclair and the City of Indianapolis? Had I lied to anyone at anytime or had I been repeatedly lied about? Had I ever threatened anyone or had I been threatened by a disturbing alliance of Community and Public leaders? Had <u>any</u> confirmation or justification of the charges against me been completed or attempted? Or did the unsupported accusations and rumors become Felony criminal charges literally within hours, based on the reputation of a vengeful Lawyer?

15

Regardless of how and why I was placed as a suspected Felon in one of the worst County Jails in the United States of America, this story is really about Faith, Redemption and the pure Gospel of Jesus Christ.

From Hearsay to Handcuffs in 15 Minutes

I spent nearly two weeks preparing for the opportunity to defend myself from these false accusations and to publically question the moral implications of a corrupt Deputy Chief of Police, outside of the State of Utah, becoming intimidated and manipulated by The Mormon Church.

My obvious ignorance of the law was surpassed only by my childish optimism that if you are honest and do the right thing, you will have nothing to fear from the Courts of Law.

I developed a thick packet of evidence and exhibits to validate my planned oral arguments specific to the massive leap between writing truthful news articles, sending accurate and informative emails and any claim of harassment, stalking, or of a credible threat of violence. The foundational issue, which I stated to the Judge, was that I had been mistreated but the Courts had been abused. Abused by a skilled attorney whose irrational initial decision to seek legal redress, was simply a reflection of his inability to deal with the real world. If no statement made by Mr. Baker was a lie, what would be the remedy? If no statement made by Mr. Baker was a deception, what would be the consequence? If no statement made by Mr. Baker was false, what would be the punishment?

I believed then as I do now, that the relevance and application of the old proverb "Perception is Reality" is most often applied exactly where and when it should not be. By this time the well-documented yet completely false statement attributed to me, *"Mr. Baker has two goals, to write a book and kill a Mormon Elder on Church property*," had been printed, reprinted, transmitted and discussed an unknown number of times. That was pure perception without even a shadow of reality. This timely piece of invented theatrics functioned very well as a diversion from my actual complaint, that a very Senior Officer of the Police Department and a respected Attorney in Indianapolis were both corrupt puppets of the Mormon Church.

A single anonymous phone call in 2009 to the Arvada, Colorado Police Department remains the only reference to the falsified statement I never actually communicated or implied to anyone, "*Mr. Baker has two goals, to write a book and kill a Mormon Elder on Church property.*"

In December of 2008, I forced my excommunication from The Church of Jesus Christ of Latter-day Saints, and began to write a book[11] about my experiences as a Mormon Bishop, highlighting the deception and deceit of that counterfeit Church. The cult of Mormonism has produced passionate, violent and fanatical members, who have taken upon themselves the extreme and irrational defense of the faith. Without question, one of the hundreds of such Colorado Mormon Church members was determined to discredit me; a member who, like I, had been sworn, on the pain of death, by a special Temple secret oath specific to the inner workings of the Church.

Although this hollow and unsubstantiated imaginary statement, as well as my background, was thoroughly investigated and several interviews were conducted by the Arvada, Colorado Police, the anonymous call and the falsified statement remain as a public record. The additional Indiana media hype soon added the phrase "*Blood Sacrifice*," which has only served to focus responsible

---

[11] Mormonism – A Life Under False Pretenses, ISBN: 978-1-937520-75-5 and LeeBaker.4Mormon.org

readers to the more accurate phrase of *"Blood Atonement"*; an actual Mormon Doctrine wherein the unrepentant Mormon apostate would have their own throat slit from ear-to-ear as part of a solemn religious practice taught by the Mormon Prophet Brigham Young himself. So common was this Mormon form of retribution that it remained as dramatic recreation within the official secret Mormon Temple ritual until 1990.

There, sitting in Court Room 21 at the desk marked "Respondent," what I had failed to grasp was the fact that I had just traveled 2,250 miles fully prepared to defend my actions without considering the next piece of the trap. I had taken the bait, knowing that I could defend my Constitutional Rights to Free Speech, but not fully comprehending that I had offended the Courts with my eight word response to Mr. Sinclair, *"Outstanding, I will see you in two weeks."* It was now the Marion Superior Court that I had insulted; specifically the Criminal Division and the Honorable Kimberly D Mattingly, Judge. For I did, without question, violate the *No Contact Order* by sending those words. Not violent words, not slanderous words, not threatening words and surely not harassing words, but words nonetheless.

Mr. Sinclair was skillful enough to let me reclassify myself from the "Respondent" to the "Offender," and himself from the "Petitioner" to the "Victim," through my own words. This did not change the likelihood that Mr. Sinclair had intimidated and manipulated the Indianapolis Metropolitan Deputy Chief of Police. My actions did not change the prospect that Mr. Sinclair had lied to the Court concerning our meetings. And finally, my eight words did not change the fact that the appalling, racist and embarrassing Doctrine of the Mormon Church, which I had distributed within Indiana, was all true and accurate.

Within 15 minutes I had pleaded my case, admitted my guilt, and Judge Kimberly D. Mattingly dismissed the case with a verbal warning and a formal ruling of "Contempt" as I did in fact respond to Mr. Sinclair. She then added, *"Unfortunately Mr. Baker, law enforcement has made me aware that there are pending warrants for your arrest here in Marion County, and they are going to take you into custody at this time."* Several weeks later, after my third court appearance, as a measure of some decency, the Chief Bailiff stopped me outside the courtroom to shake my hand and personally apologize. He said, *"Mr. Baker, I was in charge of your arrest that day. I have since read the charges and reviewed the evidence. This is a colossal travesty."*

The base evidence against me to substantiate the formal charges of 3 Felonies (Stalking and Intimidation) and 18 Misdemeanors (Invasion of Privacy) was a single email, accurately described by the State of Indiana itself as, *"attacking the appropriateness of Paul H. Sinclair being both a partner of Ice Miller LLP and an elder of the Church of Jesus Christ of latter Day Saints to co-workers of Paul H. Sinclair and/or clients of Ice Miller LLP."* These charging documents are available for your review under Cause No: 49G03-1509-F5-033343, State of Indiana vs. Lee Baker, Marion Superior Court, Criminal Division 3. I am still astonished that the very foundation of the charges brought against me by the State of Indiana are clearly centered on my repeated desire to "question" the ethics of an Attorney's association with a fanatical and racist Church. Are such inquiries illegal? Are such comparisons prohibited by law?

To clarify once again, I was in reality charged and arrested with 3 Felonies and 18 Misdemeanors, jailed and then freed on a $30,000.00 Bond, placed on a 6-month pre-Trial confinement, then subsequently monitored by two Counties from two States by GPS at a cost of $20.00 per day; all for sending informative emails.

The subject line of these emails was, *"Ice Miller and the Mormon Church – A Very Corrupt Combination,"* and it was sent not only to the clients and co-workers of Mr. Sinclair, but to the Indiana Secretary of State, the Indiana Supreme Court, the Indiana State Bar Association, the Mayor of Indianapolis, the Governor of Indiana as well as the two Senators of the State of Indiana. All of these emails were sent with a legal notice for the reader NOT to forward the information either directly or indirectly to Mr. Sinclair.

Apparently the First Amendment to the Constitution of the United States is somehow frustrated in Indiana if the topic at hand questions the integrity and conspiracy of a **Mormon** Leader with a **Mormon** Deputy Chief of Police, when exposed by a former **Mormon** Bishop. Without question the emails that I sent were thoroughly embarrassing, very accusatory and exceptionally scandalous, but not criminal. Not incorrect, not invented and undoubtedly not misleading.

It should be more than obvious to the reader as well as the Court that I have never been accused of lying about the facts, untruthful about my accusations or incorrect about Mormon doctrine, practices or teachings.

I believe that no better example of the shameful deceit and dishonesty of the Mormon Church could have been more successfully demonstrated than by the actions of Mr. Paul H. Sinclair himself. Consider this, as very senior representative of the Mormon Church, Mr. Sinclair has been uniquely commissioned and financially compensated by that organization to communicate to the Public on behalf of The Church of Jesus Christ of Latter-day Saints. As a notable Partner within the Law Firm of Ice Miller, LLP, Mr. Sinclair has likewise been uniquely commissioned and financially compensated by that organization to communicate to the Public on behalf of Ice Miller, LLP.

A reasonable person might imagine that with the combined debating skills of a senior Trial Attorney and the specialized religious training of a Mormon General Authority, Mr. Sinclair would be the <u>most</u> capable and <u>least</u> fearful of any man to address potentially sensitive questions about the Mormon Faith. Yet, this professionally trained public speaker as an expert spokesperson of his Religion, without offering a single word of coherent deliberation, panicked and ran to the State Courts for relief, refuge and remedy.

It would seem that Mr. Sinclair the "Attorney" had found some emotional protection as Mr. Sinclair the "Mormon." Retreat, Silence and Diversion are some of the more preferred Mormon strategies, followed by a healthy dose of Retribution. One of the disturbing hallmarks of the Mormon Faith is that they neither offer nor tolerate any open discussion specific to the History or Doctrines of their Faith.

Without question my embarrassing social, certainly not criminal transgression was publically questioning what Mr. Sinclair the Attorney or Mr. Sinclair the Mormon Elder did not or could not discuss privately. My now notorious email[12] clearly focused on the official Mormon Doctrines and current Scriptures that have ridiculed the Black Race, sexually abused thousands of Women and openly mocked the Government and the Laws of the United States of America.

The primary tool of the first Indiana State Court action against me was hearsay; the primary tools of the second Indiana State Court action against me were conspiracy, lies and handcuffs. With my hands cuffed forcefully behind me, five of the eleven Officers assigned the task escorted me promptly out of the Court room as the Judge moved quickly to her chambers. I had no idea that events of the following week would prove to be the most

---

[12] See Appendix B: Open Letter as Email - Ice Miller Law Firm coerces Deputy Chief of Indianapolis Police Department

desperate yet beneficial of my life. I had no idea what challenges lay ahead of me, but God did. More than just being detained at the hands of men, I was being directed by the hand of God.

County Jail, Day One – Classification of a New Inmate

The time-consuming and tedious common functions of processing new Inmates vary little from facility to facility. The recurring strip-searches, photographs, fingerprints, medical reviews, mental evaluations, segregating the violent and disruptive, integrating the common offenders and groups, feeding and then transporting dozens of men and women can be grueling. Within my first 30 hours of detainment I had been in five holding cells, strip-searched twice, fingerprinted twice, photographed twice, transported twice by van and by chain-gang three times.

The actual *Classification* of a new inmate is the administrative process of placing the inmate within the most appropriate section, division, floor or compound of the correctional facility. With my combination of Felonies and Misdemeanors, I easily qualified for 40-man open cell known as the "Gladiator Pit" on the 4th Floor. At the time I walked away from the window of the *Classification* booth, I did not know of its reputation, just holding in my hand a small blue paper, which had the innocent destination 4-b24. Now what harm could that indicate?

I slowly returned to the unoccupied communal steel toilet. I had decided that the disgusting odor and the urine soaked floor were not as bad now as they seemed a mere nine hours ago. I flushed, shook off my shoes against the wall and returned to the holding cell. With no place to sit, I stood alongside the wall. A middle-aged Latino man asked, "*Where you going, Old School?*" I replied confidently, as if I knew what it meant, "*4-b24.*" The only man nearly my age, still about 20 years my junior, laughed. "*Oh, you're screwed my friend.*" I did not want to ask why, for fear of looking weak or stupid. I already knew that I was both, but his cynical tone was still frightening.

After a long tunnel walk within a chain-gang of ten other inmates, we came to two more holding cells, stripped down to our underwear and stood in a line for the orange jail clothing. Three hours later we each were given a thin filthy foam bed cushion, a mesh laundry bag of our second set of clothing, a roll of toilet paper, and the Rule & Punishment pamphlet in both English and Spanish.

On the 4th Floor it was loud and crowded; I saw three large open cells to the right of a central Correctional Officer station behind two sets of bars with several desks and computers. After a short time in a holding cell, myself and a very large but very calm black man were directed to the last of the three large cells.

Day Two – Welcome to the Gladiator Pit

After passing through an outer and inner solid steel door with a very small but thick window we both walked past the collection of six tables. I was very careful not to disturb anyone at the tables with my flopping 6 foot mat and my mesh laundry bag over my left shoulder. Being a student of the obvious, I figured the "*b-24*" was bunk 24. It also helped that it was clearly marked as such and it was one of only two top-level bunks unoccupied. I was almost dead center in the right row of two rows of ten bunks, within a 40-man open cell with a set of six tables and one toilet at each end. I climbed into the top bunk and struggled to disregard the ear-piercing TV in a wire mesh cage just above the only doorway in or out.

It was not until much later that I learned the well-deserved nickname of that cell as the "*Gladiator Pit.*" I had completely lost track of time, but with the first meal passed through the feeding slot in the door, I assumed it was not breakfast. Standing in line to receive a meal, I was about ninth in line, yet I was the last to take a tray, as it must have been the custom for the new guy to be last. This obviously time-honored tradition was instantly understood, although it was communicated to me without a single word. Within seconds of collecting my tray, my cornbread and milk were taken and I knew better than to even glance at who owned the heavily-tattooed arm of the thief. I had once been a certified Counterterrorism Instructor, specializing in the training of Hostage Survival. I was confident that I could manage the mental harassment, but if it came to a physical confrontation, well, as predicted earlier, I was screwed.

If the intent of the Indiana Court, the Mormon Church or the Offices of Ice Miller was to get my attention and bring this disrespectful old man down a rung or two, it worked. It worked extremely well. The fact was that intimidation was the least of my concerns; real violence and brutality was a near certainty.

Much later than I expected, about three hours after the second meal (still not breakfast), I was "*visited*" by a very large man with a single black teardrop tattoo just below his right eye. Looking directly at me, he squinted a bit and spoke in a voice intended to carry across the cell. "*What's your deal, Old School, who did you screw over?*" he demanded from the side of my bunk at eye level. I answered with a slightly defiant if intentionally low tone. "*I was preaching and sent emails about a corrupt City cop and a corrupt lawyer working for the Mormon Church.*"

"*No way... that crap alone didn't get your white butt in here*" was his skeptical response. My only reaction was "*Well, it's more complicated than that, but that is the truth, I have made some powerful men very angry.*" His bold reply, now that two more inmates had come over to watch the entertainment was "*I think you are a rich Cho-Mo, Mother F and tonight I am going to beat your ass.*" With that unpleasant exchange over, I turned back to my left and faked going to sleep, although I was reasonably sure I was not fooling anyone.

I was rapidly learning what I soon came to know as a solid fact, regardless what the movies had taught me: "Hard Time" is Jail time, not Prison time. I would briefly come to know five Felons there on the 4th floor of the Marion County Jail who all agreed that the Jail time was much harder than the Prison time. The obvious reason for such a comparison was everywhere. As they pointed out to me, the explosiveness of an ever-changing population of criminals completely negates the possibility of any stability among the inmates or even among the guards.

One man boasted that his time in the Los Angeles County Jail was much worse than any Prison across the Country that he, his father or his son had been in. Without some degree of stability the hierarchy and power pyramid of the inmates is fluid and chaotic. Without the stability of a semi-permanent inmate population, access to personal property, recreation time, individual hygiene and medical attention is frenzied at best.

I do not advocate or suggest that the conditions at the Jail or the treatment of the inmates are wildly disproportionate to their crimes, not at all. In fact, the majority of those I came to know willingly admitted their guilt and did not protest their incarceration; they only wished to return to Prison at the earliest possible opportunity. It seemed that being in Jail was considered the "Wild West" of the Correctional Community and once inside the Inmates were truly in charge.

My specific objection is that once a person is merely accused, then his treatment, punishment, safety and confinement is precisely that of the convicted. Without evidence, investigation or trial, the accused (me) is subjected to exactly... absolutely precisely the same punishment as the convicted. If the allegations and charges are falsified then the accused must seek redress at his own expense. I submit that in my case, a high-power Mormon Lawyer whom I embarrassed and humiliated, truly mistreated me, but he completely abused the Public Courts.

Again, the movies were wrong. I was never given the opportunity for a free phone call. I was not informed of the charges against me prior to being locked-up and I was never provided my daily heart medications. Even after 6 months of pre-Trial confinement, my movements were severely restricted and I was still GPS monitored at my expense ($600 per month for a high-tech ankle bracelet), but following some personal research, the real depressing education came at the end of 2015.

After spending nearly $30,000.00 on totally fabricated charges, I remembered what several Inmates and one Guard explained to me, on the realization that I was not the normal *"client."* The Legal, Justice, Law Enforcement and Correctional Systems in America were more of a cooperative Private Industry than a Public Service. It surprised and depressed me to verify through 7 major statistical resources that it was true; The United States of America incarcerates more citizens' per-capita than any other Country on earth, and by a wide margin. I had become a statistic, a client, and a customer, but sadly the Public was not better off as a result of my participation in this expensive and degrading charade. The phrase "Presumed Innocent until Proven Guilty" was now just a ridiculous and wishful description of a Free Nation that had died to me.

Within a few hours Mr. Personality, the self-appointed President of the Hospitality Committee was back at my bunk for round two. This time, the subject was money and my pin-code for the cell-block phone. With a collection of new observers this time, his demands began in earnest. *"I want your old lady to send you some money for me."* And *"I want your phone pin right now Cho-Mo."* The phone pin is given to each inmate to make outgoing monitored calls on a pre-paid account; this is set-up and paid for by someone on the outside in conjunction with the inmate's pin, which is only to be used by that specific inmate.

By the grace of God, at that exact moment, my name and bunk number came over the cell-block speaker system. "*Baker, B24, Medical, be ready.*" I climbed down from the solid steel bunk and could feel the glaring eyes follow me as I weaved past the group, making sure not to touch any of them or make any eye contact. When I made it to the still locked door, I did not turn around but I clearly heard the threat, "*Later Cho-Mo, Later.*" I stood at the door, head down like a puppy waiting to be walked outside to take a pee.

Soon a young guard and an older trustee opened the door, "*Baker?*" I nodded yes. I was chained and handcuffed and we were off to the Medical clinic. I was told on the way that all new inmates to the block were to be photographed and screened by Medical. I later learned that this procedure would "document" my current condition. It seemed that the "condition" of many Inmates could mysteriously change after some time in the "Gladiator Pit." Imagine that. Down the hall I went, into a holding cell, then out again and down another hall past what looked to be the guard's central command area behind two rows of bars. After one more holding cell, I was escorted into the Medical clinic and took a seat.

After a few minutes I calmed down and just relaxed on the first cushioned chair I had been on in several days. I prayed that my wife, Kathy, was holding together under this pressure. It was nearly an hour before I was seen, but that gave me time to consider the truly bizarre deviation my life had taken. How and why did this happen and could I recover from it?

Not many years ago I spent several days at the CIA Headquarters representing the National Security Agency on a joint Covert Operation that had gone badly. It was true that we had worked out the technical issues, but a repeat of the human failures, on our part, would guarantee an internal investigation that could compromise the ultra-classified multi-million dollar covert Program. What had happened to me? I had once worked on the White House communications strategies and Nation's electronic deception techniques.

But now, I was delighted just to sit on a chair with a thin cushion. In a not so distant past life, as a respected Intelligence Analyst, I remember hosting several Congressional visitors at the CIA and NRO Museums, as both were highly classified and within the respective Headquarters secured locations. On the other hand, the NSA Museum is open to the public, which makes it more accessible but greatly reduces the true capabilities and operational techniques that can be on display.

Painfully aware of whom I once was, I sat there in silence. The only person in the room in Jail orange and in chains, I just stared into space half-listening to the Guard, the Nurse and the Trustee chatter on about some insignificant office politics and how nice it will be when an un-named supervisor would finally be on vacation. Nothing really spiteful, just normal office complaining. I was struck by the highs and lows of my life, of the massive contrast between my current situation and the several events in my past life that I might have considered as major achievements. This was personally demoralizing.

As I contemplated exactly what this "medical examination" would require of me, I thought of my Counterterrorism Training with the Special Forces Unit at Fort Bragg, North Carolina, and how the Hostage Survival portion of the training was the last time I found myself in handcuffs. That was the spring of 1985, I was 29 and in the best shape of my life. I knew that my current environment was not "training" and, with an additional 30 years and 30 pounds, my psychological capabilities were not going to be particularly useful. I considered this experience the absolute lowest point of my life.

I drifted back to one of the high points in my life, just prior to a transfer to the National Security Agency's Denver Office on Buckley Air Force Base. I had spent 45 minutes alone with General Keith Brian Alexander, Director of the NSA. In view of my current situation, that day back in May of 2006 provided me with a short, yet totally worthless, reminder that I was once considered a true American patriot and a respected professional. We had then reminisced about old times, past co-workers and simpler times when the Intelligence Community had clearly defined enemies and achievable objectives, each supported by massive budgets. I am sure I had a strange distant look and a senseless half smile when I was snapped back into reality. *"Mr. Baker, I am ready to see you now."* What was this, *"Mr. Baker?"* The pleasant and respectable tone did not seem appropriate considering my surroundings. Not appropriate at all.

The night-shift Jail Nurse for the "Gladiator Pit" was a thin older black woman with a kind smile. Still, I was sure something bad was going to happen. She had a skinny brown folder open on her desk and asked me, *"You really have no record, no prior arrests or convictions?"* I answered with a firm but polite, *"No Ma'am, this is the first time."* She took my blood pressure and asked if I was on any prescription medications. I told her of the three daily prescriptions. She interrupted and asked, *"Do you normally have high blood pressure?"* I responded with, *"No, never."* I felt I could trust her, so I told her that I had been accused of being a child-molester by several very large Neanderthals in my cell and that I fully anticipated a beating later that night. She pointed at a small white cross on a ring on her right hand, and asked, *"Are you Ok with this?"* That gesture began a silently choreographed conversation where she slowly asked very deliberate questions, with direct eye contact, as if expecting me to provide coached answers. I immediately understood and respectfully asked for whatever help she could offer. She could tell that I genuinely did not know the

29

exclusive procedures, processes or techniques for simple survival in Jail, much less within the "Gladiator Pit."

With the unspoken clarification and explanation of the seriousness of my situation, I asked for Protective Custody, not fully understanding what that meant. She reached for an additional set of papers from a wall-mounted file and asked the Guard to come to her desk. With a very detached tone she reported, *"This inmate has requested for Protective Custody."* The Guard, now joined by the Trustee asked, *"Is this true? Why?"* Without any hesitation I answered, *"I have been threatened and I fear for my life."* Extremely aggravated he responded, *"Ok, you got to tell me who, you must show me who threatened you, you got to file a formal complaint with his name on it and then SIGN IT!"* He stood up and said, *"You are going to point him out to me, right now!"* Just then the Nurse added, *"That's it, I am ordering PC for this inmate, and that is the end of it!"*

I was escorted back to a holding cell, and there I watched a parade of Officers and Guards pointing and staring at me. Within 30 minutes, I was again returned to the open cell and went and sat on my bunk. Just as I lay down to fake going to sleep, the announcement came over the speaker, *"Baker, get packed, be at the door."* The walk across the full length of the open cell from my bunk to the double doors was incredibly intimidating. I wanted to wait with my back against the first of the two doors if only to limit my exposure to any attack. They all knew intuitively that I had requested out. Eight maybe ten men stood in my way without moving. I did my best to dodge each without any contact. With my Jail clothes jammed in the laundry bag under my left arm and my bed cushion under my right arm, head down, I weaved my way among the brutal comments and rock-solid pillars of seething hatred. I would soon learn that my short but intense walk of shame and humiliation through the "Gladiator Pit" was a God-send.

Three Guards unknown to me were at the second door within 10 minutes, although it seemed like half an hour. The final remarks and insults were amazingly profane and graphic. I heard *"roll on one,"* then a deep metallic click, *"roll on two"* and the first door was open. I was once again chained and I shuffled between two of the three Guards. One more hour in a holding cell, the very same cell that was my first stop on the way to the sweet angel of a Nurse whom God had placed on the night shift to save me from an unimaginable night of terror and violence. Alone, I could relax; I dropped my filthy blue cushion on the cement floor and I stretched out. The time passed much more quickly, I had my laundry bag for a pillow and I was able to use the toilet for the first time without an audience or any offensive comments. With no toilet paper, if there would be an inventory at the end of my stay, I was going to be one sock short of my full clothing issue, if you know what I mean. But I was alone and life was getting better. Better by the minute.

Day Three – Locked-up 23 hour a Day and Loving It.

I heard my name but it was in a distant conversation, then two Guards approached the cell. The taller one was swinging a pair of handcuffs, while the other dangled a mass of keys in one hand and held a few papers in the other, *"Let's go... we got you a cell"* As the taller Guard began to pull my arms behind me, he was told, *"In front is fine, we are not going far."* Then I was told, *"So, we got the mug shots from the Pit. You need to show us who threatened you."* My assumption was that they were just jerking me around to see if they could get me to point someone out, and then hassle Mr. Personality back in the Gladiator Pit. Understanding the weight of the phrase that the Nurse had used, I countered with, *"Not a chance, you can take me back if you want, but I am formally requesting Protective Custody."* Without knowing precisely what I had just asked for, my mind raced with some very unpleasant options. Was protective custody a padded cell? Was protective custody a small steel room

31

without bars? Or was it going to include a straight jacket or some other additional restraint?   We walked only about 200 feet or so down a thin gloomy corridor. At the far end was a steel door with a small window. Through that door was a second identical door, then a row of cells numbered 1 to 15. The Guard with all the keys opened a black control panel and yelled, "*Roll on 10!*" He flipped two red switches and I was escorted to my cell. With the handcuffs now off, I picked up my laundry bag, which had stuck to the filthy floor.

Several conversations were going on well above the noise of the TV, which was set inside a cage within a cage and hung above the second door. It was so loud and the conversations so enthralling, I was not noticed, or maybe it was that I was not to be noticed. Either way, I spread down my single blanket and just kept quiet. Even an inexperienced first-timer like me knew that the "*New Guy*" only speaks when he is spoken to.

I had, not surprisingly, developed a vicious case of diarrhea, and I actually looked forward to my own toilet, knowing that once I had cleaned it, it would be reasonably safe. Within only a few minutes I heard a voice far off to the left call out, "*Who just came in?*" My first assumption was that this group was the men who did not play well with others or could not follow the rules. I was wrong, but I would not know that for the first 24 hours. The man to the left of me was in an entirely different Prison uniform. His large black and white stripes indicated a Federal Inmate down to the State Courthouse for a hearing or trial. In any case, he told me to answer the question so they would shut up about it. "*I am the new guy, name is Lee Baker.*"

After that I felt like a fish out of water. It was hard to believe, at nearly 60 years old I was still playing head-games with myself. Should I say more? Should I just sit down and shut up? Should I tell anyone my story? I had to slow down and just unwind; there was no rush for any information to be blurted out as no one had really asked. I sat and listened to the incredible blend of complaints, jokes and sports analysis for over three hours. Regrettably, I now know more details about a woman on the west side of Indianapolis than even her husband knows. I managed to fall asleep for what felt like only a few minutes, but it must have been several hours due to my exhaustion and lack of daily medications.

To keep my head away from the potential reach of anyone near the bars, it was a simple choice to sleep with my feet out and head up towards the wall. The price for that small margin of security was to have my face only 7 inches from the toilet. Even using the simple one-piece Jail toilet proved to be a new skill that I was sorely deficient at. Without fresh air, a new Inmate with an active digestive track would obviously want to make and disperse any donations as swiftly as possible. I would soon learn that all special Inmates within my current accommodations could only use two flushes per hour. Pushing the button as often as I would, nothing happened. Without the need to ask if I had a defecation problem, Ricky, next door to my left, unsympathetically commented, *"Cover it with your towel. You only get two flushes per hour."* I said, "Thanks," covered my toilet with my towel and thought to myself, *"You did a fine job on that First Impression. Nice... real nice, Lee."* It was obvious that I was new at this and that I had a lot to learn.

The first meal from the thick blue plastic tray was served and I just kept quiet. No complaints, no trading, and thankfully no awful cornbread to choke down. The Jail issue included a thick plastic spoon and a cup that I used to mix the orange drink powder. I placed the empty tray back on the feeding shelf and attempted to flush the toilet. It worked, so an hour must have passed.

The diversity and volume of the conversations were truly remarkable. Listening closely to the names called out around me, I worked out at least three groups of common interests centered on the primary subjects of sports, computer technology and music. A fourth sub-group skillfully traded amazingly dirty jokes from one end of the cell-block to the other. I heard Mark, Rick, Dirt, Black and what sounded like just the letter "L" The vast majority of the Black Inmates just simply used the "N-word," which made me uncomfortable as I had always been very critical of the Mormon use of that word. Housed at nearly the center of the group, I could comprehend both the TV and semi-follow the intense argument about the best Bands of the 80's at the other end of the block. I had absolutely nothing to offer on any of the subjects and I was very comfortable with that current arrangement. In any case, it would have been rude to join in. Imagine that, I was briefly evaluating a potentially rude action in a place where violence, brutality and aggression are the absolute norm.

Eventually, my immediate neighbors to the left and right did superficially introduce themselves to me. They were only slightly interested in my implausible story. I got the very distinct impression that they were not at all concerned about my personal analysis of the circumstances; they only wanted to know the charges, just the charges. I let any amplification or justification go for the time and just plainly stated, "*Felony Stalking, three counts.*" With that I was off-stage for the rest of the day. I dialed back my marginal interest in the several conversations, put on my second T-shirt and fell asleep. I was relatively safe; safe in that no one could just show up at my bunk or shove me over a table from behind.

Day Four – Setting the Foundation: The Gospel of Jesus Christ

With no "lights-out" like in the movies, the only all-purpose way to tell time was by the three meals or if someone on the line asked a "*Chota*" for the time. Chota is one of the many sarcastic names for the officers or guards, way too close to "*Chomo,*" the name I had been called earlier in my stay. Even then, using the meals as an all-purpose clock, it seemed that mealtime could range some three or four hours from when anyone would expect it. I think

34

our group was last on the meal runs as the other open-bay cells housed as many as 40 Inmates and the meal cart looked nearly empty each time we were fed.

In any case, it was early and still cold when Dirt called out, *"I got an egg for milk."* I sat up and saw the cold blue plastic tray on the feeding shelf of my cell; I had missed its delivery by Ricky, who was the man "out" and making the runs for food trades between the cells. The row of 15 individual cells were numbered 1-15, left to right as viewed by any inmate within a cell. Number 1, to my far left, was closest to the door, TV, shower and small table. With only one man "out" for only 1 of the 24 hours, it took almost three days to actually see all the inmates with whom I had been speaking.

I was in cell 10. Alec Clark or "Dirt," a professional paint and construction Supervisor was in cell 8 and the only individual who gave me his full name and address, although the others provided adequate Social Media contact information. Mr. Ricky from the Federal Prison (black and white striped jumpsuit) was on my left in cell 9. To my right, Mark from Tennessee was in cell 11. "L," the well-traveled intellectual of the group, resided in cell 13; and Vangelo or "Black," a computer programmer, was at the end of the line in cell 15.

There is no point in discussing their individual crimes beyond the fact that all were repeat offenders and Felons, some holding multiple convictions over many years and most guilty of violent crimes to include murder.

The man "out" walked in front of each cell in a walkway, more of a dog-run about 60 feet long and 6 feet wide, which was within a second set of bars. During the periodic Officer Welfare visits, headcount or the dispensing of medications, all inmates were locked down with no one in the secured small walkway.

Once more Dirt called out, *"Hey, Lee, you want another egg?"* It was nice to hear my name and not *"Hey Old School."* It was a small thing, but it meant that in some way after four days of hell, I was a bit more of a person again. Without any hesitation I acknowledged the offer. *"Ya, I'll take an egg for milk."* Just then Black yelled from far right, *"Egg for cornbread!"* Never a big fan of cornbread, I sealed the second verbal contract and in no time Ricky had made the swap. I was the proud owner of three cold hard-boiled eggs and some chilly oatmeal, which no one wanted.

After about 30 minutes, Ricky collected the 15 trays, one of the responsibilities of the man "out" during meals. He carried some trays and kicked the rest along the floor down to the waiting guard or trustee. Being "out" during meals gave you the chance to pick extra food off the trays of less-sociable inmates who kept to themselves during the regular trading of food. The man "out" for his one hour was also the primary vehicle to trade books, food, paper or any item between cells.

With breakfast now done and the next man "out" on the phone beneath the TV, Dirt in a much lower tone asked, *"So, Lee, really... No BS, you are here because of a stupid religious problem?"* I took a deep breath and instinctively answered, with some embarrassment, *"Well, it's one of them long stories."* It was a stupid response, but Dirt eased my awkwardness with a quick reply in his southern drawl. *"Well, damn, tell me about it ... unless you are on your way somewhere that we don't know about."* Mark, now back in his cell, lightly chuckled as if we all were old friends on a fishing trip and I had just fallen off the back of the truck.

I don't know why I was uneasy about the prospect of summarizing my current situation. It might have been just how completely out of place I had felt for the past four days. What I had done was not criminal or violent. Back in high school days it would have been considered foolish, a self-inflicted wound, offering no real gain. A "Bush League" act.

Seriously, each of my cellmates had been tracked down and beaten into submission after a long and violent string of offenses. On the other hand, on the day of my arrest, I had a pleasant spaghetti lunch with my wife at noon, bought a pack of gum, crossed the street to the Court House and spoke to the Judge for 15 minutes. I then found myself bent over a desk in chains for sending truthful religious emails and preaching about Jesus Christ.

Although my own assessment might have been very accurate as "Bush League," the fact was I was now deep in the "Major League" and in a very bad place with very bad men. Just two days prior to this unique opportunity to share my faith with Dirt, I stood in chains next to Mark Leonard, a man guilty of felony murder. This 46-year-old psychopath blew up his Indianapolis home for the insurance money and destroyed or damaged 80 other homes, killing newlywed neighbors John and Jennifer Longworth, who were trapped in the resulting fire. He was convicted and sentenced to two life terms plus 75 years without the possibility of parole, and I was on the 4th floor in Jail with him. I had a stained protective custody single cell down the hall just like him. I was dressed in orange just like him. And I was in chains just... like... him. I have no doubt that it was the primary sinister objective of Mr. Sinclair, the Offices of Ice Miller and the Leadership of the Mormon Church, to so over exaggerate the charges against me, as to place me within precisely that type of dangerous situation.

One would think that a semi-rational middle-aged man without any criminal record or history with the Law, finding himself in this perilous situation, might have thought to himself, *"Something is wrong, something is really wrong, why am I here?"* And yet, when the opportunity to share the Gospel of Jesus Christ with several men I had never met before came, I felt oddly comfortable.

My fellow inmates were still puzzled as to just why and how I would be jailed for a non-violent Religious dispute. More than that, Dirt specifically asked, *"Lee, how are you a suspected Felon over some e-mails if they did not communicate a threat?"* I told him it really was not **how** I questioned the subject of religion; it was more **who** I had directed the questions to. Mr. Paul Sinclair is a very rich and powerful man. I am sure that his pride, reputation and influence are normally not questioned, tested or ridiculed. Dirt added, *"I just hate how religion is the cause of so much that is wrong with this world. Its everyone's damn religion, twisted every way possible that is the foundation of so much evil."*

Speaking to Dirt, but knowing the others were listening, I asked, *"What specifically do you have issues with?"* Without much hesitation he replied, *"Well, ya see... I grew up with Church, but never really trusted the Bible."* Our deep-voiced southern inmate from Tennessee, Mark, the only true short-timer there, as he was simply awaiting transportation back to the West Tennessee State Penitentiary, lightheartedly mocked, *"Shoot-fire, that there book ain't even in real English is it?"* Ricky did not add to the exchange, but I heard him laugh a bit.

Given a few more minutes of foundational questions with Dirt, I clearly saw the two essential issues for him were, *"Why Trust the Bible?"* and *"How bad is just too bad for Jesus to save you?"*

Later that day I would reflect on just how surreal that whole exchange was. The three and sometimes four of us continued our conversation amid the blaring of the TV and several other conversations on the cell block. Vangelo or *"Black"* was fervently delivering a presentation to *"L"* specific to some new computer program that enabled some old *"data mining"* technique to do something in some way that was just remarkable.

Up near the front, somewhere among the first 5 or 6 cells, another trio was discussing the finer points of girls, guns and some poor fish in G.P. Like everything else that week, I understood only half of what I heard and not much more of what I saw. It turned out that the *"poor fish in G.P."* was a new inmate that got beat bad two nights before over in one of the General Population cells. Apparently, life on the 4th floor was faster and cheaper than anywhere else in the facility.

Within less than an hour I could, as the others already had, completely tune-out the other conversations which echoed off the wall in front of us. Routinely, amid all of the apparent chaos, the man "out" at the time might join one or two conversations simultaneously. Then in the far walkway beyond our area an Officer or Trustee might walk by and, without missing a beat, a few of the inmates might shout out *"Sir, got the time?"*, *"Sir, done with that paper?"* or *"Sir, could you ask for my case manager?"* Most often the Officer or Trustee continued without any acknowledgement whatsoever concerning the several requests, to which the inmates might offer a special and graphic farewell gesture or two.

Three and a half days of confinement within a remarkably intense, strange and violent place will certainly fine tune your survival skills. Until I was challenged to first tell and then justify to murderers and thieves my absurd story of preaching to the Mormons, I was concentrating on achieving the most inconspicuous and submissive behavior of my life. I spoke only when spoken to, I never made eye contact, and I never for anything! Discreet observation and inconspicuous concealment were my only focus. Now, relatively safe in my own small one-man cell and only "out" 1 of each 24 hours, I could reduce my anxiety and fatigue to compensate for my lack of three "old man" prescription[13]

---

[13] Metoprolol Tartrate 50mg, Zetia 10mg and Fluoxetine Hcl 20mg

medications. Although I had been entirely focused and totally content to blend into the background, it was not to be.

But to share the pure Gospel of Jesus Christ, without first criticizing and condemning the many deceptions and dishonesty of Mormonism, could I do that? As an enthusiastic amateur Biblical historian, having spent some study time in Jerusalem, I felt very confident that I could present a rational argument to trust the Bible. In point of fact, the fortunate and unique opportunity to discuss Dirt's two issues, with little or no interruption, was essentially a very sad statement on the current pace of my life.

My first task was to establish the credibility of the Bible, not only as the Word of God, but as a historically accurate and linguistically trustworthy document. I began with a few examples of some truly impressive statistics unique to the Bible. These examples were intended to demonstrate that because of its message, audience and age, the Bible stands alone as the most well-preserved ancient document of all time. Without some historical background, it is understandable how most people would easily believe that such an ancient document, given its many translations and transcriptions, could be corrupt in some way, either by sheer probability, pure accident or dishonest intent.

Given my "captive audience" (pun intended), I was able to take my time and build some comparative examples that really resonated with our small group, especially with our representative from the deep South, Mark, who would occasionally swear in disbelief.

I started where I was most comfortable, in the history of the Bible. As an avid enthusiast of all things historical, I have always enjoyed sharing and witnessing the flash of connectivity when a person comes to the recognition that they are an integral piece of human history.

40

Unlike in the movies, there is no "lights-out" time in Jail. Something is always happening and the lights are always on. It seemed to me that more inmates were asleep during the day than in the evening. I only mention it now because near the beginning of my first illustrations as to why the Bible can be trusted, Dirt yelled out, "*Hey, L, you hear this?*" With no response, Mark helped out from the right side with "*L, you up?*" Still no response. L, a graduate from Duke University was fast asleep. It was interesting how these men could tune out the blaring TV and the several other conversations and still participate in a second or third debate or just sleep through the entire circus.

In any case, while listening to the conversation, Dirt was hooked; he understood the example I had used to demonstrate that the Bible was nearly impervious to any major changes or corruptions over the years. Or at the very least if there were to be any changes, they could be identified through comparison and association. I had told the group that, aside from the fact that I loved history, I had been fortunate to have toured and studied in Israel. One of the more vital lessons I had learned first-hand was the true significance of the sheer number of ancient copies of the Bible. Over 10,000 incomplete copies or fragments of the Bible have survived from literally every corner of the known world in the 2nd and 3rd Centuries A.D.

The events I asked them to consider were the unique circumstance at or just prior to the destruction of Jerusalem by the Romans in 70 A.D. This is when the majority of the Christian community had, under significant oppression, left the beleaguered city and Judea in total. With them went copies of their most valuable possession, the letters from the Apostles and followers of Jesus Christ. Without exaggeration, the two Jewish Wars against Rome, the first 66-73 A.D. and the second between 132 and 135 A.D., were the most significant events in all of history specific to the proliferation and precision of the Biblical New Testament.

I detailed how the fierce persecution of the young Church demanded a mass exodus to distant lands. From the very epicenter of the new faith they frantically dispersed. From Jerusalem to Jericho they fled, from Capernaum to Corinth they were on the run. Into Egypt, Macedonia, Spain, France, Italy and as far away as Britain they scattered, bringing with them the copies of the letters from Paul, Peter, Matthew and John. Within three generations of faithful Christians, what had been a collection of several dozen copies in a single region of the world became several hundred copies dispersed across over four thousand miles.

I explained how truly violent and intense the Roman hatred for the Jews had become. In 70 A.D. the Roman General Titus completely demolished the Temple that Jesus once knew, which took King Herod 80 years to complete. Then, with the second Jewish revolt in 132 A.D., the Roman Emperor Hadrian himself reduced Jerusalem to little more than rubble. The Romans had spent more time, more money and more manpower on the Jewish Wars than they did in subduing any other Nation, Civilization or Rebellion. The retaliation of Hadrian remains impressive by any standard. He renamed Jerusalem to Aelia Capitolina, he renamed the entire region from Judaea to Palastina, in honor of the mortal enemy of the Jews, the Philistines. He made it illegal for any Jew to live in the region and required that Jews worldwide pay an annual tax to build and maintain the Temples of the Roman Gods.

Even today, the names Palestine and Palestinian are reminiscent of the vengeance of the Roman Emperor Hadrian almost 2,000 years ago. I mentioned to my State secured and seriously supervised Jail students that within formal Jewish literature and among the majority of the Jewish elite, if the name of Hadrian is ever spoken or written it is always followed with the phrase: "*May his bones rot in Hell.*"

After a short break for the library cart and the exchange of more books, we began again. I was impressed to hear that someone unknown to me, up in cell 4 or 5 asked for a Bible from the lower shelf of the library cart. I came to understand that inmates on this floor could have only one book and a Bible. Just then I remembered a very insightful internet question that went something like: *"Why is it that our Children cannot read the Bible in School, but if they go to Prison or Jail... We will give each of them one?"*

Having driven home the point that the Romans did an impeccable job at ensuring the total Jewish and Christian displacement, sometimes known as the Diaspora, we could move on to the core subject. I shared with the group that it was my belief that God had a hand in the violent dislocation and remote dissemination of what would become the New Testament. My conviction was based on the fact that such a wide-spread and long-term dissemination of copies of the inspired text would ensure that any additions, deletions or changes would be plainly obvious when compared to the total group of surviving scriptures.

Dirt got it immediately and Mark was only seconds behind him. As if stage-managed by God Himself, Rick then asked if any examples of changes or attempted changes existed to prove that point. I rewarded him with, *"Great question, You get my next cornbread."* Now with at least four Bibles on the Cell Block, I asked the men to turn to the Book of John, Chapter 8. Above the roar of the TV, I heard "L" call out, "Where is John? I got no tabs." That made five Bibles on the Block. Mark, nearest to him recited: *"Matthew, Mark, Luke and John."* We were ready for the first practical exercise in why the Bible is trustworthy.

When everyone was at Chapter 8, I asked if they saw the small note in brackets just above the beginning of the Chapter. Among all the positive answers, "L" came back with, *"No, I don't see any note in brackets, just the beginning of the Chapter, why?"*

Mark joked, "*You're get'n to be a problem Slick!*" I added, "*No, that is a good thing, we can use that in a minute.*" I then read the note in the brackets that most of us had within our Bibles, "*The earliest manuscripts and many other ancient witnesses do not have John 7:53 – 8:11*"

I then explained that the purpose of this note in the Bible was to let the reader know that within the original Greek Manuscripts of the Book of John, the well-known story of the woman taken in adultery did not exist in the original hand of John the Apostle. Further, I described the fact that this was altered after the widespread use of the printing press with movable typeset in about 1450. Prior to that all Bibles were hand-copied. It is most likely that the event itself is true; the undisputed fact is that it was not originally written by John.

With this realistic demonstration of a minor theological inconsistency from a current printing of the Bible finished, I was now able to complete the following mental image. If, either by pure accident or corrupt design, any change was introduced to the Bible it would be easily identified when compared to the thousands of older manuscripts. The unintentional but incredible safeguard to the text of the Bible was secured by the fact that 1st and 2nd Century A.D. copies were in use by Christians separated by thousands of miles and in diverse cultures. They understood how this condition guaranteed absolutely no possibility of a coordinated modification to the original copies of the letters and manuscripts that would soon become the Bible.

As an example, under such circumstances, if a change to the Book of John was initiated by a rebellious Christian Monk or Scribe in Egypt, it is now possible for modern scholars to compare and identify any changes. Such inconsistencies have been discovered in comparisons to the thousands of copies of the Book of John, in

Greek, from faithful Christian congregations in Italy, Spain, and England or among the Germanic Tribes.

Add to that, the incredible fact that the Dead Sea Scrolls, containing most of the Hebrew text of the Old Testament, date back to approximately 160 B.C. and were skillfully preserved with insignificant changes. Additionally, as a strong point of corroboration, these ancient Old Testament Scriptures were actually read, accepted, quoted and practiced by Jesus Christ Himself.

So, back to the issue noticed by "L" that not all Bibles alert the reader to possible inconsistencies within a particular version of the Bible. In anticipation of a potential question and to gauge the effectiveness of the lesson on the impossibility of a rogue Monk or Scribe altering or deleting Doctrine, I asked, *"Ok, before we clarify the difference between a Version of the Bible and a Translation of the Bible, do you boys understand the point that the Bible text is about 98% free of manuscript errors and 100% free of any false Doctrine?"* A voice called out, sarcastic yet lighthearted, *"Who you be call'n a Boy, Mr. No Ink, Old School Cracker?"* But they understood. They really did. It was critical to set the foundation, even though I couldn't see it in their eyes, that any further discussions about God, Jesus or those religious fuzzy things, the Bible must be trusted.

The uniqueness of the Bible is paramount and vital to understand. I explained that the Bible has been the most studied work of literature in all of human history. We discussed how the Bible has been validated and revered as a historical guide, an archeological guide, and a cultural guide by millions who couldn't care less about its religious significance. Specifically what sets the Bible apart from any other ancient text can be summarized in three simple categories. One major strength of the Bible is found in the consistency of the text, the uniformity of the text and the accuracy of the text. Over 10,000 ancient copies or fragments of the Bible exist for study, review and comparison. The primary events, characters, locations and battles of the Bible have been validated from non-Biblical records (Egyptian, Assyrian, Babylonian, Roman and others) that would have had no motivation whatsoever to either corroborate or validate the Biblical narrative. Yet, the most distinctive and validating characteristic of the Bible are its hundreds of prophetic statements.

The Bible stands alone among all other Religious Documents (The Qur'an - Islam, The Tripitaka - Buddhism and The Bhagavad-Gita – Hinduism) due to its multitude of accurate prophetic statements. The statistical likelihood of predicting specific details and conditions of exact events to named locations, nations, events and persons is astronomical.

The final step was to explain to my fellow inmates the difference between a version and translation of the Bible. Without question, this single issue has proved to be a major stumbling block to many because, on the surface, it would appear that the numerous versions of the Bible communicate either a wide range of messages or even contradictory accounts of God, Jesus and those religious fuzzy things. It was the afternoon of Saturday, September 26th. The man "out" was on the phone and our impromptu Bible study was about to be interrupted.

The cold, thick plastic food trays arrived from the far right just as the man "out" on the phone, at the far left, began yelling and screaming obscenities. Apparently, his wife or girlfriend had some difficulties transferring funds to his phone card. I did not recognize his voice and from my cell, I could only see his orange jumpsuit reflected on one of the three windows just past the second row of bars. The trustee pushing the rack of food trays was accompanied by a massive bald black guard who must have been 6'6". He ordered the now furious inmate to get off the phone and back into his cell. The unknown inmate slammed the phone down and very resolutely yelled, *"I am going to kill that bitch."* The guard and the inmate then exchanged a rapid fire of graphic insults. We stopped our conversation and waited for chow.

I sat at the end of my bunk, in silence, without the pressing requirement to formulate my next point concerning the foundation and function of the Gospel of Jesus Christ. The smell of urine, the senseless blare of the TV and the sound of the toilet flushing next to me reminded me exactly where I was. I was over two thousand miles from home in a very cold, very violent Jail, facing 3 serious Felonies and 18 Misdemeanors. Lunch passed without a word and oddly there was no trading or complaining about what looked to be a stroganoff of some kind. With two fingers and a simple *"Hey,"* I passed the never-ending piece of cornbread through the bars to Ricky. *"Thanks Man,"* he said, and the seemingly mandatory silence continued.

I had the impression that it might have been too much too fast, or that it was simply enough for now. As I lay down and just listened for what seemed like three or four hours, I felt more of an outsider than ever. I was never told to let it be, it just seemed like the thing to do, as the next set of conversations did not intentionally exclude me, but they were certainly over, around and beyond me. I withdrew as the subjects ranged from drugs to women to sports and then back to women. This was not a bus stop or a public restaurant. At nearly 60, I was embarrassed that I could not ask them to clean up their language. It was as if my small group that was sincerely interested in God and the Bible needed to reconnect with the other inmates for a time.

It felt like everyone there knew that I was the short-timer and at that moment it was best to take a break from my Bible stories. It felt particularly discouraging to have held their attention on such an important and uplifting subject one minute and in the next to witness such a depressing and vulgar exchange between two men, whom I would soon propose that Jesus loved equally.

I considered that I might have represented a unique opportunity for the group, especially for Ricky and Mark who had nearly 18 years each to complete at the Federal Penitentiary. Unique in the sense that they unquestionably knew of and had ready access to "Born Again Inmates" or "Jesus Freaks," but perhaps I was outside of their own well-defined and judgmental groups. Another hour or two passed.

Just as I was thinking it should be my time "out" within the next few hours, Dirt asked, "*So, Lee, you up...Why are there so many different Bibles?*" I quickly rose in my stocking feet only to realize how sticky the cement was; I did not even want to guess at the combination of fluids that had caramelized on the floor, so I just slipped on my orange Krocs and stepped to the bars. "*Good question.*" I spoke as if just to Dirt, hopeful that the others would listen as well. In the style of a cheap lounge comedian, I restarted the conversation with a joke, "*So, Dirt... before I had these religious issues with Mormons, my psychiatrist told me I was crazy and I said, no way... I want a second opinion. He said Okay... you're ugly too.*" And with that we were back in business.

I began with the acknowledgement that there was in fact a great number of versions of the Bible available and that they seemed to be marketed so that anyone could find a version that they were most comfortable with. The implication is that these "versions" are all different and that these "versions" all disagree with each other. This is a very common but incorrect understanding. I struggled to remember the details of a chart we used in our Bible Study, which illustrates the fundamental differences between these "versions." Even among some Churches, the versions of the Word of God harvest only minor opposition given the fact that they vary only in style but not in content. No literary version of the Bible, ultra-

48

Orthodox or ultra-Liberal, actually makes additions, changes or deletions to the core Biblical Doctrine. I made it clear that it was the Doctrine of the Bible that should be sacred and revered, and not the style or splendor of the language. I remembered that the best way to describe the core differences between these "versions," several of which we had with us in Jail, was that the more Conservative version can be considered a "Word for Word" translation and the more Liberal or Modern versions can be considered a "Thought for Thought" translation. That is to say that all, or most of these "versions" begin with the original Hebrew, Greek and Aramaic manuscripts and attempt the best translation for the intended audience. I gave Dirt a simple illustration that it is generally accepted. That is, the New International Version (NIV) of the Bible is very much middle-of-the-road, within this continuum of Biblical "Versions." I added that the Living or Message Bible was at the far Liberal (or Thought for Thought) end of the scale and the Interlinear or New American Standard Bible at the far Conservative or (Word for Word) end of the scale.

This extreme marketing strategy will certainly compromise some of the finer points of the many cultural nuances and further degrade the loss of "word-power" and "word-meaning" already destroyed by the process of a "Translation" itself. Yet, without question such literary styles and progressive marketing has put the Bible within the hands and hearts of many millions who could never have found much empathetic comprehension in the King James, 1611 version of the Bible, given the Old English language.

The best Biblical example of this that I could remember was the often used word "Love." I shared this with the group, which I knew to be expanding when I heard at least Ricky and "L" make sarcastic comments to let us know they were back. In English, I explained, we have only <u>one</u> word for "Love," in contrast to the Biblical Greek, which has at least <u>four</u>. I used the well-known "**If**

you love me, feed my sheep" message as the example. I was grateful that no one asked me to give the Scripture reference, as I knew the story but not the reference. I now know it can be found in John 21:17. Feeling rejuvenated, I continued on with the example, *"Okay, here is the best example that I know of to demonstrate the loss of the passion and precision of a single word during a translation."*

When Christ asked Peter if he "loved" him, the significance of the Greek word used is massive and the implications of Peter's response are heartbreaking, but the spiritual drama is completely lost in English. Jesus asked Peter, *"Do you [Agape] me?"* Agape is a special sacrificial love almost unique to Christians. Peter's answer communicates a less-than-total devotion: *"You know that I [Phileo] you."* Phileo is a friendly, more common brotherly love. The point here is that in English, our only option is "Love" and the drama, passion and commitment of the moment is totally missed. In Greek there are two other words for love, *[Eros]* is for sexual passion, and *[Storge]* is used to describe the love between a parent and child. In English, the use of the word "love" demands additional context and explanation if any special or exceptional implications are to be communicated.

I love my wife very much and I love chocolate very much; both are grammatically correct statements, yet these declarations clearly demonstrate the limitations of our language. When the full potential of a "lost in translation" reality is multiplied by extremely important Religious, Cultural or Intellectual requirements needed to accurately translate a thought or event, then one truly understands that there is much more danger in a careless "Translation" than in a casual "Version."

I gave a few more examples of major historical events, precisely recorded within the Bible but not critical to the Bible narrative, like Kings, Rulers, Battles, Locations, and World-events. I felt the initial confidence in the Bible was finally secured among our small group. Ricky was particularly interested in the unique agreement between non-Religious Archeology and the accuracy of the Bible. Specifically, he was impressed with the period of the Biblical King Hezekiah, the Biblical Prophet Isaiah and the Assyrian King Sennacherib, as well as the events in and around the fortified Cities of Jerusalem and Lachish (720 B.C. to 701 B.C.) His interest in these precise events may have been slightly influenced by the two-hour dissertation I provided him while the others were lamenting that the Cavaliers had no defense at all and the Patriots just plain sucked. Those were subjects that both Ricky and I could care less about.

With the milestone of teaching how and why to trust the Bible behind us, the much more important question of just who Jesus Christ really is, could be discussed in the morning. It was late, I was tired, no one was going anywhere and football remained the dominate discussion as I fell asleep. It had been a good day, and it had been so uplifting to set a foundation around the Bible that I knew would be critical in tomorrow's preaching of the Word of God. Today the message was biblical history, cultural antiquity and individual stories. Tomorrow would be the personal application of the most important message ever communicated between humans, the Gospel of Jesus Christ. Somehow that night, it did not smell as bad as or seem as cold as it had the night before. I asked Dirt to check the schedule and to please skip my time "out," to pass it to the next Inmate after me, as I was sure that I could sleep more than four hours. Other Inmates routinely had more pressing reasons to get to the phone and I had already planned to call Kathy on my next time "out." It was a good day... in fact, it was a great day.

Day Five – Teaching the Pure Gospel of Jesus

I was deep asleep; I had almost forgotten where I was. "*Move something Baker, let's go!*" I sat up just in time to see a Guard with a clipboard pass. It was a welfare check to ensure the next team of Guards got as many live Inmates as were on the official count for the previous team of Guards. Suicides, murders and overdosed Inmates were not uncommon. I would later learn that at least one and frequently two deaths a month were completely expected. And with that, a somewhat bizarre yet completely routine event, designed to ensure that I had not been killed or taken my own life, day five in Jail began.

The group seemed extraordinarily quiet and for a minute I could not remember if it was Sunday or Monday. In the lull of the morning, while scanning my cell for graffiti, I noticed that the walls had been recently painted the same dull grey but only up to the height a man could reach without a ladder. Just at the new paint/old paint line on the back wall, I noticed a scratched word or two. At the right angle, just above the old paint line I could see the words "*for me,*" and under the new paint and much less obvious was the word "*Pray.*" I wondered under what conditions those words were etched into the walls of this cell and how long ago they had been placed there. Without my medication I felt noticeably more melancholy and on edge; nevertheless I silently offered a short prayer for the man who had left those few compelling words.

I had laid back down for only a few minutes when the "man out" called for chow. There must have been a change in the delivery pattern of the meals as this was the first and only warm meal of my stay. It was small scoop of bland but warm oatmeal, and yes... cornbread. The "man out" and I had not yet met, but he knew of my dislike for the yellowish brick of sawdust. As he pushed my tray through the feeding slot of the bars, he already had his hard-boiled egg in his right hand and without the need of a formal request; I just nodded and said, "*Okay.*" With that, the yellowish brick of sawdust was gone and my meal was at the moment good enough. With two eggs again and still no pepper, I just had to ask... "*Any of you ladies got some pepper?"* Mark, in a sarcastic southern drawl, instantly joked, *"Forget the pepper, when you find that lady you are ask'n about, you send her on down here, you hear me, Boy?"*

After chatter back and forth about some crazy College Basketball score that no one could believe, and I couldn't care less about, I began to gather my thoughts on the task at hand. I knew, that within the next day or two I would be out on Bond. Before my incarceration, I had never thought about needing to say the words, *"out on Bond,"* but it was true.

I silently prayed and then asked Dirt to turn to the first chapter of the Book of John. I asked him to mark the page with his finger, then close the Bible and listen to a few things I wanted him to know more about what we were going to read. I told him that no man has or will ever have the power or the ability to convert anyone to Jesus Christ. I promised him that if he would isolate, just for a moment, this magnificent conversation from this horrific environment and then cradle within his heart a small measure of faith, the Spirit of God would touch him.

At first I did not know if Ricky, who was in the cell between Dirt and me, was awake or asleep, so I spoke in a soft tone. I described how I had come to find a limitless and unshakable inner peace in the very words that we were about to read. I told him that my unwavering faith in these words was not the result of some terrible event in my life that had caused me to desperately search for some unfathomable cosmic answer. I told Dirt how the Spirit of God, did, in fact, come to me through these scriptures, with such clarity and tranquility that my entire being was forever and immeasurably changed.

I paused and explained that the concept of the unconditional Love of God and the Gift of Salvation through Faith in Jesus Christ alone had come to me during two very distinct and divergent periods in my life. Incredibly to most Orthodox Christians, my wife and I had actually both come to know and love Jesus Christ from within Mormonism, more accurately from within our time associated with Mormonism. I further qualified that statement for Dirt and now Ricky, with the following explanation. After over thirty years as a Mormon, it was only during the last four or five years that I was challenged to defend or explain the peculiar Doctrines of the Mormon Faith. Doctrines so many have considered un-Christian and un-Biblical.

The primary reason that members of the Mormon Faith are ignorant as to the details of their own Church is the massive and well-coordinated effort of the Mormon leadership to rewrite, republish and rework both the core Doctrine and the Historical records of the Mormon Church. This enthusiastic determination to constantly "mutate" Mormonism from within the Church has given rise to the very fitting if sarcastic label, "the Chameleon of Christianity."

The second, but equally important factor is that The Church of Jesus Christ of Latter-day Saints is less than 186 years old. This seemingly insignificant detail has plagued the Mormon Church with the unenviable distinction of a consistent and reliable paper-trail of the words and deeds of their founding Fathers. The total number of early Mormon historical records, scriptures, manuals, sermons, diaries, newspapers, revelations and official pronouncements and declarations is astonishing. The relatively young and uniquely American Mormon Church has, fortuitously for the honest of heart, been established during a period of history in which many original and unbiased records and primary source documentation can be researched and studied.

The third critical element of specifically how the "older" Mormon generations "could" or "might" have claimed religious ignorance was the relative inaccessibility of those tens of thousands of early Mormon documents in the past. Until only a few years ago, it would have taken a truly monumental effort to find and read, much less correlate and cross-reference those documents. With the advent of the computer and the internet, almost anyone can review, often from the official Mormon Church website itself, how many young girls or wives of other men Joseph Smith Jr. had sex with or how many sanctioned "Nigger" jokes have been told by the all-white Mormon Apostles during their revered General Conference meetings. Accurate Mormon history is now the single most powerful adversary of the Mormon Church and it is the principal reason that the Mormon Church membership is in a steep decline today.

Just then Dirt grumbled a bit. *"On with the story... **please**... my finger is turning blue."* I conceded to his point, but added the final self-exoneration, *"Gentlemen,"* I clearly stated, *"It was my own fault, I simply did not know Mormon Doctrine, and because of that I did not know that the Mormons really believe that **God** was once just a man like us and that **Jesus** merely is the older brother of **Satan**."* I spent only a few more minutes describing my complete exit from Mormonism and then I clarified that it was the offensive and blasphemed nature of the "Mormon Jesus" that truthfully motivated my departure. The Jesus Christ I had come to know and love was **not** the Jesus of Mormonism and I felt both ashamed and profoundly depressed that my ignorance had carried my four children into this Cult.

And with that the stage was set to have all three and possibly more (although I did not want to take attendance just then), to turn back to the Book of John. I then asked my small group to consider three short but very profound statements of truth: God Loves You, God Knows You and God Accepts You as You Are Today.

As we turned to the Scriptures I was compelled to place the first chapter of John within a larger Biblical framework, by highlighting the fact that the Apostle John makes a very deliberate reference to the Book of Genesis, while establishing the unity and oneness of God with Jesus. I began with verse 1, "*In the beginning was the Word and the Word was with God, and the Word was God.*" Without discussion, I asked my new Brothers in the Gospel to move directly to verse 14, "*The Word became flesh and made his dwelling among us. We have seen his glory, the glory of the One and Only, who came from the Father, full of grace and truth.*" I took that extraordinary moment to just let those remarkable words drift across the several cells, and then I asked, "*Given this clear and distinct recognition that the Word is God and that the Word became Flesh and He dwelt on this earth as Jesus Christ, can you comprehend the enormous value of the actual words, teachings, and actions of Jesus Christ? If that Jesus is the exact and perfect representation of the One True God, the very Creator of all things seen and unseen within all creation?*"

Nothing was said for a short time and I immediately questioned myself. Had I become overdramatic or too theatrical? Was this potentially life-changing and insightful conversation too out of place against the background of the TV blaring a Bud Light commercial and two other inmates laughing at a filthy joke? Dirt was the first to speak, "*I had never made that connection before.*" I added, "*Not only is Jesus, God in the flesh, the Creator of all, He knows every intimate and private detail of you, and He loves you as you are right now, here in this Jail.*" I continued with a brief overview of the most essential and core element of the Gospel: The Love of God.

I asked for Dirt, Ricky and "L", calling them by name this time, to turn a bit deeper into the Book of John, in Chapter 3, verse 16. By this time Mark was up but had not yet joined the conversation. I could see half of his left arm extended beyond the center bars of his cell. I slowly and deliberately read, "*For God so loved the world that he gave his one and only Son, that whoever believes in him shall not perish but have eternal life. For God did not send his Son into the world to condemn the world, but to save the world through him."*

As I closed my copy of the Bible and laid it on the worn and damaged feeding shelf built into the center of the cell door, I said, *"Let me close with this thought."* I projected my voice straight ahead this time to maximize the reverberation from the long grey brick wall in front of each of us. Just then a Guard passed to the left on the outside track as the "man out" passed to the right on the inside track, both totally oblivious to our very public, yet exceptionally private conversation. I told them how, to God, each one of us was perfectly equal in every critical aspect of our lives. That God, because of His great Love for us, has not planned for our failure through some complex network of tests, trials and competitions. Quite to the contrary, He has planned everything for our success, everything for our victory and everything for our triumph. I declared with confidence that all that God has promised us is available through our Faith and Belief in Jesus Christ alone. I explained that the entire Bible, every parable and every promise, points to the person of Jesus Christ as our Savior, our Redeemer and our Lord.

After some thoughtful silence and to lighten the mood without being discourteous to the Spirit of God, I closed with these words: *"Take some time... take some serious time to think about the monumental significance and the amazing potential of this message. Know in your heart that regardless of what you and I have done in our broken and sinful lives, we can never, ever earn or work our way back to God or into Heaven. Your belief in Jesus Christ alone as Lord of your life is paramount to all other issues. If you have any questions, stop by. The door is open and we can talk... remember to wipe your feet. I have just taken some cookies out of the oven and I have a tall glass of cold milk waiting for you boys. "*

I was both exhausted and exhilarated. I had rarely, if ever, shared the Pure Gospel of Jesus Christ without building my defense upon the complete destruction of Mormonism. What God had just shown me was that I should not ever mingle or weave His message of Love with my intense desire to expose and destroy Mormonism.

Day Six – A Change of Perspective

On the morning of my last day in Jail, I began with time in Prayer and in the Word of God, specifically in 2 Corinthians, Chapter 11, verses 12-15. Several years ago this scripture spoke to me as I was being questioned about my obsessive efforts to discredit the Mormon Faith. I felt then as I do now that one only needs to know the details of Mormon Doctrine, to demonstrate that this faith is one of the most cultish of religions. This is why my preferred audience has been the educated and intellectuals among the Mormon Leadership. I have been fascinated by those who are able to segregate their intellect along the lines of rational thought for their profession and still maintain that Joseph Smith Jr. was completely justified in repeatedly sleeping with another man's wife and then lying about it. My single goal has only been to ask Mormons to own Mormon Doctrine.

I am very secure in my position that no rational, moral or ethical person could both know Mormon Doctrine and then aspire to have that same Doctrine, given all its implications, knowingly govern the lives of their Children. It is the ownership of the Mormon Doctrine by the Mormons that I seek and its outrageous and irrational comparison to the Christian Doctrine that I despise. The view and passion of the Apostle Paul concerning a counterfeit devotion is perfect indeed,

> *"And I will keep on doing what I am doing in order to cut the ground from under those who want an opportunity to be considered equal with us in the things they boast about. For such people are false apostles, deceitful workers, masquerading as apostles of Christ. And no wonder, for Satan himself masquerades as an angel of light. It is not*

58

surprising, then, if his servants also masquerade as servants of righteousness. Their end will be what their actions deserve." **2 Corinthians 11:12-15**

The early part of the day seemed a bit frantic. Dirt was the man out after morning chow and on the phone when I woke from a short nap. He came by my cell about half-way through his hour out and told me that he had just talked to his wife about our *"Bible Study"* the day before. He extended his right hand into my cell, we shook hands, he looked me in the eyes and he said, *"I believe it, I believe it all... I really do."* I asked if he had accepted Jesus Christ in the way we spoke about. *"Yes, I have."* A sheepish smile came across his face and I could tell he could not manage much more of the sensitive stuff. *"Now what about those cookies you promised?"* he asked. As if a child, I hung my head and said, *"Well... ya see, the thing is... I was lying about that."* In his heavy Southern twang Dirt said, *"Looks like I need to talk to you about Jesus."* He smiled and walked away.

I was almost certain that I would be released before lunch, but just to gain some insight I asked Ricky and Mark, *"So... do they have a certain set of times for daily releases?* Mark enthusiastically provided an overview. *"Okay, first you need to understand that you skip your last meal in here."* I thought he was joking, *"Really, why?"* Ricky added, *"It is just bad luck, it really is."* Then Mark resumed. *"You need to realize that get'n out is more of pain in the ass than get'n in. It may take 6 to 8 hours, and you need to divide up your cantina and property as you can't take anything out."* Well, I had no personal property and no food items to be concerned with, so I asked, *"What do you mean?"* Ricky offered some clarification, *"Split up your toilet paper, blanket and socks among us, and I could use a second cup. Also, did you get any Tylenol or Aspirin from the Nurse?*

I was way too much of a beginner to have much in the way of parting gifts, but I did ask Ricky if he needed anything done on the outside. He just said, *"Pray for me, I have 16 more years and I do not know if I got it in me to finish the time."* I told him I would pray for him and then I added that a deep and lasting peace could be found in the Bible. He said, "*I know... I did not miss a single word of your lessons, but Lee, I have done some really bad shit.*" I could not see him, but I knew he was close to our common wall and towards the front of the cell, "*Repent Brother, repent and accept Jesus alone. He loves you as you are. Seriously, it is not a payback. That is man's way to even the score. But His way is a total surrender, a total submission, a total belief... no score.*"

Just then, the pace of life on the 4th floor of the Marion County Jail accelerated rather abruptly for me, but I am sure it was viewed as just another day by the two Guards ready to serve us lunch and the unseen Administrator whose voice bellowed over the speaker, "*Baker, pack-up, be ready.*" The man out was a stranger to me and he was visually taken back a bit when I declined my lunch tray. "*Take what you want, I am leaving today.*" Without any hesitation, the mighty cornbread was gone, Ricky took the two turkey patties and Mark got the milk.

It is my assumption that as a final insult from the Mormon collaborators or more of a perverted demonstration of control, I actually remained in Jail for four-days **after** my Bail was paid. The well-documented fact is that Kathy posted my Bail at 1:00 p.m. on Thursday the 24th of September and I was not released until after 5:00 p.m. on Monday the 28th.

It was nearly an hour before I heard the rattle of the keys and the electric power switches at the far end of the bay. Then my cell door slid to the right and I heard the final order, "*Baker, let's go, you're late.*" As if I had any degree of control of my schedule, I snickered and grabbed my stuff. I first went to my far right to give my blanket to "L" who had been complaining about the cold for days. I actually sleep better in the cold and I should have given it up earlier, but I assumed, as is noted on the Jail property sheet, "All lost items will be paid for." She was very touched and grateful for the extra blanket.

It should be completely understood that "L" was only marginally interested in the earlier Biblical History lessons and even less concerned with the "*Love*" of Jesus stories. In one of those peculiar coincidences that can change lives, my wife Kathy and I had actually met and spoken with "L" a few months earlier in the shadow of the Mormon Temple, where this legal nightmare began. Totally unrecognizable to me, "L" normally presented herself as Lillian Oblivion, a well-educated and articulate medical student with one of the most agreeable personalities I have ever encountered. I believe that she had been placed within my path for two very important reasons, my growth and her healing. Listening to "L" day after day, I had pictured a thin, somewhat refined and very white college student. In reality, she was nearly toothless, heavily tattooed with very delicate features.

I was embarrassed and humbled by my irrational assumptions and judgment. Lillian had been a deep-tissue facial cancer survivor and severely sexually abused as a child within foster care as early as age 6. I am so glad that she did not judge me by my external associations but rather by my testimony and love of Jesus Christ. Originally from Romania, Lillian had been repeatedly beaten in Georgia and South Carolina by fundamental Christians for supporting the LGBT community. As I handed her my blanket, she said, *"You are one of the only followers of Jesus that has actually demonstrated to me His love within my life."* As the Guard was shaking his handcuffs while yelling at me to hurry, my final words to Lillian were, *"Please know that Jesus really... really does love you."*

I quickly passed out my remaining toilet paper, a T-shirt and a few other items, and I was gone. I then began the arduous process of discharge and pre-Trial confinement, knowing that those six days were intended for an evil purpose to intimidate and humiliate me, but that God had turned it to His good, His glory and my growth. My personal resolve to continue the lawful and accurate exposure of the deception and deceit of the Mormon Doctrine remains undaunted.

I have matured in my belief in Jesus Christ and I have grown in my compassion for my fellow men. I have personally both seen and documented the corruption and dishonesty of the several Officials charged with the sustainment of the Law and the Trust of the Public, I now more jealously and conscientiously value my freedom. And yet, I value the Word of God more as I rest in His Peace, Grace and Mercy.

A Corrupt Court in Collusion with Ice Miller, LLP

I should explain at this point, exactly why I would not only consider but eagerly accept any Plea Agreement from the State of Indiana, if I truly felt that I had not committed a crime. The answer is simple, it comes down to trust and confidence in the legal system, and I have none. I am certain, beyond any doubt that I would not have received a fair trial or a fair sentence given the over exaggeration of my actions, the embellishment of the charges and the amplification of the required punishment.

I believe that the first written Plea Agreement[14] presented to me from the State of Indiana has served as an exceptionally accurate representation of the fundamental motivations, associations and unethical intentions of those involved in this travesty of Justice. The State Prosecutor's vindictive requirement for me to have absolutely no contact of <u>any</u> kind, regarding <u>any</u> subject with <u>any</u> client[15] of Ice Miller, LLP for <u>any</u> reason, is both unprofessional and the best evidence of either legal incompetence or unrestrained retribution.

Understand, no written Plea Agreement from the State of Indiana has ever been issued to me with any indication that any one of the several different Plea Agreements was a draft, a version, or an outline. The fact is, I could have simply signed the very first written Plea Agreement from the State of Indiana, fully accepting the truly absurd limitations required by the Prosecutor. I believe that these limitations were specifically crafted to protect the reputation of the

---

[14] See Appendix C for the Original Plea Agreement offered by the State of Indiana
[15] See Appendix A for a partial list of the over 500 clients of the Law Firm of Ice Miller, LLP.

Law Firm of Ice Miller, and limit the embarrassment of the Mormon Church.

Following are only a few examples of what would actually, literally and legally constitute an in-person violation of the first Plea Agreement from the State of Indiana. Any of the following seemingly insignificant actions would have certainly placed me in "Contempt of Court." Based on the State's Plea Agreement, normal everyday contact with any of the over 500 clients of Ice Miller, would reinstate the three Felony charges and ensure Prison time:

1. I am a full-time resident and tax payer of the State of California. If I attend a class for Biblical Studies offered at San Diego State University, I would be in "Contempt of Court." San Diego State University is a client of the Law Firm of Ice Miller, LLP.

2. If visiting my mother in west Denver this spring, I were asked to pick-up her arthritis medication at the local Target Store, I would be in "Contempt of Court." The Target Corporation is a client of the Law Firm of Ice Miller, LLP.

3. If our current home water filter became clogged again, and I called our local Culligan service representative, I would be in "Contempt of Court." The Culligan Water Company is a client of the Law Firm of Ice Miller, LLP.

4. If, on the way home from Church, I were to stop at our local McDonald's for a Big Mac, fries and a Coke, I would be in "Contempt of Court." The Mc Donald's restaurant Corporation is a client of the Law Firm of Ice Miller, LLP.

5. I am a member of the Wyndham Hotels and Resorts. If on a trip to the coast of California, if I were to use my Membership Points for a single nights stay, I

would be in "Contempt of Court." The Wyndham Hotels and Resorts Inc. is a client of the Law Firm of Ice Miller, LLP.

6. If after my night's stay at the Wyndham Hotel, I were to purchase sunscreen at the local Wal-Mart Store in Monterey, I would be in "Contempt of Court." The Wal-Mart Corporation is a client of the Law Firm of Ice Miller, LLP.

7. If on the way home my car needed some minor repairs and I were to stop at the new Ford Dealer in Los Banos for a head light, I would be in "Contempt of Court." The Ford Motor Company is a client of the Law Firm of Ice Miller, LLP.

8. If I could not pay for the headlight, desperately needed on my car and I went to my Bank, the US Bank in Los Banos for a loan, again, I would be in "Contempt of Court." The nationwide US Bank Corporation is a client of the Law Firm of Ice Miller, LLP.

I could go on with these juvenile but legally valid examples of how the State of Indiana had grossly overreached in its authority to suppress me, to protect the Law Firm that represents the City of Indianapolis as well as attempt to limit the embarrassment of the Mormon Church. And if I were in fact to send a short one-page complaint about this treatment to the Indiana Chamber of Commerce, from my home here in California, I would actually, literally and legally be in "Contempt of Court" again, for they too are a protected client of Ice Miller.

Earlier, I openly ridiculed Mr. Paul Sinclair as a Partner of Ice Miller, LLP, specific to his inability to submit legitimate charges against me and also for using the Courts as his personal weapon of retribution. I now openly scorn the Prosecutor for the State of

Indiana for issuing a Plea Agreement, which I believe clearly demonstrates an egregious overreach of his authority. Do these Attorneys not know that the very words and phrases that they so casually issue have the potential to damage or destroy lives? Do these Attorneys not understand that the very words and phrases they so carelessly distribute to the Public are only moments away from the unquestioned authority and legally binding power of a Judge?

It is very possible, even probable that the Prosecutor, who authored the Plea Agreements for the State of Indiana, did not literally intend *"no contact of any kind with any of the clients of Mr. Sinclair's employer."* Such a statement would clearly indicate that I could not purchase a Big Mac, or stay at a Hotel or pick-up sunscreen or even call the "Culligan Man." to fix my water filter. But, obviously the State Prosecutor is an educated man, skillfully trained and certified to represent the citizens of the State of Indiana, so, my assumption is that he both knows the Law and knows the English language. As such, I should not speculate or hypothesize on what the State Prosecutor meant to communicate, or what he intended to write or what he really wanted to say.

Or is it possible, even probable that when I sent the short e-mail response to Mr. Sinclair stating, *"Outstanding, I will see you in two weeks."* not knowing the Law as the State Prosecutor does, not knowing that those eight mild-mannered words were legally in "Contempt of Court." Or is possible, even probable that was not what I meant to communicate, or what I intended to write or what I really wanted to say. After 6 days and nights in Jail and $30,000.00 later, I would suggest that I have truly felt the consequences of my actions, mistakes and careless behavior. And yet, if I as a common citizen recognize and then criticize some legally binding, if extremely abnormal limitations formally required by the Prosecutor, he can just change a few words and hit the print button again. No harm, no foul and no responsibility or consequence to the State.

The last minute insertion to the formal No Contact Order adding the Utah based Mormon Church (The Church of Jesus Christ of Latter-day Saints) is a bit more problematic. Here the State Prosecutor forbids any contact, in any form, on any subject to a worldwide Organization that, heretofore has not even filed a complaint or motion with the Court. Additionally, a search of the Court records does not reflect any grievance or objection communicated by The Mormon Church to the State that would require or even suggest the need or condition for The Mormon Church to be added to the Plea Agreement. It is very unlikely that the State Prosecutor would on his own sincerely feel compelled to enhance the Plea Agreement with such a subjective item, if not so motivated from an external source.

After dealing with the obvious favoritism and corruption within Indiana for over 6 months, my return to an State Criminal Court would not be sensible or productive. I would have no expectation of fairness and the exposure of this story would only be frustrated and delayed by the expenditure of additional funds with no prospect of justice. As such, the State of Indiana's offer to administratively reduce three Criminal Felonies to three Low-level Misdemeanors, seems a bit mystical but very attractive.

It clearly is not enough to satisfy the State of Indiana, Ice Miller and the Mormon Church that I have been falsely accused, wrongly incarcerated, that my firearms have been confiscated, my every movement monitored and so severely restricted that I have been denied vital Medical attention and Cancer screening for 6 months. The offered Plea Agreement was in its original form, simply spiteful and absurd by any legal or ethical standard.

My opinion is this: to win in such a Court would be both very unlikely and very expensive. Yet, bringing this True Story out of the Court and into the Public will result in a much higher probability of exposing the collusion and corruption, which will in turn increase the probability of any real change to the improper and incestuous relationships within the Indiana Courts. I sincerely believe that this demonstration of ruthless legal action is being stage-managed in Indianapolis by the Leadership of the Mormon Church, through the Mormon Deputy Chief of Police as well as the Law Firm of a very powerful Mormon Attorney.

Justice is Not Blind - At least Not in Indiana

On Thursday, February 18th of 2016, the partly overcast sunrise at 6:46 was stunning, but it was a bit chilly in Indianapolis at only 45 degrees with a moderate wind from the southwest. No major activities were planned within the city that day and, other than a few minor traffic accidents, the Police were still looking for Nathan Wayne Johnson, a medium build black man suspected of robbery, whose last known address was in the 3700 block of North Tacoma.

One very significant and remarkable event in my world would go totally unnoticed by the good citizens of the City of Indianapolis, which was founded in 1820. Coincidently, 1820 was the very year that Joseph Smith Jr., the founder of Mormonism, claimed to have had a visitation from God Almighty in upstate New York and then completely failed to let anyone know about it for 12 years. I have often wondered how a personal meeting with God Himself, if that story were trustworthy, could have been taken so lightly as to *not* warrant even the mention of such an event to anyone, even his family, for over a decade.

In any case, just before noon an extraordinary legal maneuver placed the citizens of Indiana back into a more secure situation. My two Felony charges of Intimidation were dismissed, simply dismissed. The written order which came with that news included a brief explanatory statement, *"The facts as stated do not constitute an offense as charged."* Signed, Judge Sheila A. Carlisle and Commissioner Stanley E. Kroh, both from the Criminal Division of the Marion Superior Court. Without a Plea Bargain, without the presentation of any evidence or additional information, without a trial or an apology the charges were just... gone, vanished... dismissed, as if they never existed.

I was obviously delighted and clearly depressed at the same time. For six months I had been a suspected Felon. For more than six months I lived under the very real intimidation of knowing that the National average for a first-time conviction of Felony Stalking is 3 to 5 years in prison. My severe frustration centered on the simplicity and casual nature of the explanatory legal statement from the Judge, "*The facts as stated do not constitute an offense as charged.*" Did the facts change? Did the facts six months ago constitute a "real" offense yet now they meant nothing? Was the legal and authorized swift movement of a State Government to incarcerate a man, potentially for several years, really that arbitrary?

Only a week later I was offered a somewhat ominous opportunity to seek a "one-time" Plea Bargain. The explicit offer was the dismissal of the final Felony Stalking charge in exchange for 3 Misdemeanor charges to include some form of non-reporting Parole for 3 years. Considering the fact that for six months I had been on a 24-hour GPS monitor and a pre-trial travel restriction to just one county, I was sufficiently exhausted and they knew it. I was advised that the State had always believed that this case should have been within the Civil Division and not the Criminal Division. The probability was, to save face after issuing 3 very serious Felonies and 18 Misdemeanor charges, the State of Indiana could **not** just let me walk away totally unpunished.

Supported entirely by many gracious donations, just over $30,000.00, my rapid, expensive and painful education in the true cost of freedom and justice was more than adequate. Without the Plea Bargain I was facing a possible 3 to 5 years in Prison and an additional cost of at least $10,000.00. After some sage advice from my Attorney, warning me that this case could <u>still</u> land me in prison for 3 to 5 years if the jury did not comprehend the details of the case, I surrendered to the reality of my situation and humbly returned to Court to accept the deal. Sixty years of life without an arrest record, a Disabled Veteran of 36 years of dedicated service, I felt cheated. But, I begrudgingly accepted my punishment that was dished out by the Citizens of the State of Indiana.

After fully six months of some very costly pre-trial confinement, incarceration and theatrical legal strategies under the very real threat of several years in Prison, the final details are incredibly bizarre.

Two formal charges of Felony Intimidation were written and submitted to the Marion County Superior Court by Mormon Elder Paul H. Sinclair, a senior partner of the Law Firm of Ice Miller, LLP. Subsequently, both charges were **dismissed** by the Court with the following explanations:

> *"The allegations run afoul of a line of cases in Indiana and will not support a finding that the defendant intended to place the victim in fear of retaliation for prior acts."*

> *"The Court therefore GRANTS the Motion to Dismiss as the facts stated do not constitute an offense as charged."*

And the last Felony charge was no more valid than the first two, which had completely vaporized under even a marginally competent legal review. The last Felony charge was held <u>only</u> as a motivation for me to relinquish my struggle and provide some measure of dignity and purpose to both the Court for such an egregious overreach of authority and to Mr. Paul H. Sinclair, representative of the Mormon Church for his vengeful incompetence. I have accepted the lesser of two evils and I will take the Misdemeanors and remain on Probation for the next three years.

I now have a criminal record, but I am certainly not ashamed of it or how and why it was earned.

I suspect that the Law Firm of Ice Miller and or Mr. Sinclair himself will now pursue a retaliatory civil court action to stop the publication of this story. I would further surmise that although I may carry the emotional and physical scars of this ordeal, the wide distribution of this story would not encourage the current or stimulate additional clients to such representation.

It is true that I do not personally know of Mr. Sinclair's complete history as a properly trained and licensed Attorney in the State of Indiana. Yet it is my opinion and I can state with some authority and experience, he is the one of the very best examples of the lack of ethics to be found within the Mormon leadership, the lack of integrity to be found within the Mormon leadership and the abundance of deception to be found within the Mormon leadership.

My two-part question is this: With the very real risk of me spending several years in Prison, how and why did the Court ever accept these formal charges in the first place? Were these unsubstantiated and vindictive charges accepted merely on the reputation and position of a partner of the Law Firm of Ice Miller?

Were these two Felony charges of Intimidation just simply not written well enough? Were these charges simply not justified by the facts? Were these charges simply not researched? Were these charges simply not supported by additional case law? Were these charges simply not true? Or where these Felony charges of Intimidation issued out of pure frustration with the intent to cause me physical, emotional and financial harm?

And what were these Felony charges based on? I would ask the reader to remember that within the Charging and Arrest documents issued by the State of Indiana is the following accurate statement for which, I do admit total responsibility: *"attacking the*

70

appropriateness of Paul H. Sinclair being both a partner of Ice Miller LLP and an elder of the Church of Jesus Christ of latter Day Saints to co-workers of Paul H. Sinclair and/or clients of Ice Miller LLP."   Yes, I did send a number of probing questions to Government, Regulatory, and Professional Organizations, both public and private to question the "*appropriateness*" of the integrity and character of a fellow human being. Was that a crime? Was that a felony? Was that deserving of severe punishment?

And how does this incident reflect on the professionalism of the Law Firm of Ice Miller, who represents the City of Indianapolis and its Police Department, which have been implicated in this corruption? If... if these several Felony charges were completely dismissed for cause, and issued by a first-year Student of Junior Community College, that would be tragic but completely understandable. How is it that a senior partner of the powerful and respected Law Firm of Ice Miller, could so causally and yet so ineptly risk my welfare for his personal retribution?

At our home in California on the morning of Wednesday, the 2nd of March 2016, I received a completely outrageous and excessively oppressive Plea Agreement[16] from the State of Indiana. To both demonstrate and confirm the unethical and corrupt connection between the State of Indiana, the Law Firm of Ice Miller and the Mormon Church, I have included a copy of that document within Appendix C. The "Plea Agreement" from the State offered to dismiss "all" remaining charges, if I would agree to Never Discuss this Story[17], Never Report this Story, Never Publish this Story, Never Comment on this Story, Never be Interviewed about this Story and Never Contact the Mormon Church, on <u>any subject</u> and in any manner, means, method or mode for three years.

---

[16] See Appendix C: Plea Agreement – State of Indiana v. Lee Baker

[17] With any of the millions and millions of Americans associated with any of the over 500 clients of Ice Miller, LLP.

My juvenile overconfidence and unchecked passion combined with Elder Paul H. Sinclair's pride and embarrassment escalated into a daring and dangerous misuse of the Courts as a personal tool of retribution. How absolutely vengeful and yet completely and characteristically "Mormon" this entire event had been.

I had been beaten, physically, emotionally and financially. And yet, I had been given a very personal, precious and unique, if somewhat risky opportunity to preach the Gospel of Jesus Christ to a group of men I would otherwise never have known, within an environment I would never have experienced.

With the clearly demonstrated and well documented widespread corruption within the City of Indianapolis, my center of gravity, specific to any past respect or reverence for the legal system, had changed forever. After 36 consecutive years of dedicated service to the Nation, I knew that I would never again regain my trust or confidence in the Rule of Law. I had experienced first-hand what millions before me had dealt with either by the nature of their finances or the color of their skin. "Justice" in Indiana is **_not_** blind and her favoritism **_can_** be prolonged, persuaded or purchased.

My intent was never to physically threaten Elder Paul H. Sinclair. So apparent was that fact that "On-the-Record" and in the Courtroom, Judge Stanley E. Kroh stated, *"Mr. Baker, I do not believe that you ever intended to harm Mr. Sinclair, but in this world, people get scared."* A very accurate observation but somewhat pointless, as he had just 10 seconds earlier convicted me of three Class A Misdemeanors and dismissed three Felony charges worth 3 to 6 years of my life.

My only intent was to intellectually challenge Sinclair's integrity, question his knowledge and dispute his statements as a nationally-recognized, highly-qualified and well-paid representative of the Mormon Church. I do sincerely pray that Mr. Sinclair might come to a more complete understanding of the History, Doctrines and Practices of the Mormon Church. I pray that he and his family might be blessed with a sure knowledge that Salvation is based on a Personal Faith and Belief in Jesus Christ alone and not in the buildup of Works, secret Handshakes or the desire to become a God. I give all honor and glory to God for the occasion to teach and preach of Him and of His Son through His Holy Spirit to those behind bars.

And finally, I give Thanks to God for His grace and for His mercy in turning what was obviously designed and crafted by deceitful men as a punishment, into a blessing and an opportunity for my personal growth and maturing in His Holy Word. Amen.

In His Service,

Lee B. Baker

The Mormon Church has a long and well-documented history of sanctioned revenge killings of its apostate members. In the unlikely event of my accidental or otherwise questionable death, I would ask that The Church of Jesus Christ of Latter-day Saints and those individual Mormons identified within this book be seriously considered as suspects.

March of 2016, Former Mormon Bishop - Lee B. Baker

Mormonism and Utah

A brief review of

National Statistics

Sources:

Salt Lake Tribune, CBS News, Centers for Disease Control and CNN

Utah leads the Nation in **On-Line Pornography**

Utah leads the Nation in **Teen Suicides**

Utah leads the Nation in **Anti-Depressant Drug Use**

Utah leads the Nation in **Child Sexual Abuse**

Utah leads the Nation in **Unprosecuted Rape Cases**

Utah leads the Nation in **violent and abusive Polygamy**

Utah leads the Nation in **Deaths by Drug Overdose**

Utah leads the Nation in the **Bankruptcy Rate**

Matthew 7:16

By their fruit you will recognize them. Do people pick grapes from thorn bushes or figs from thistles?

Appendix A

Listing of the Major Clients
of the
Law Firm of Ice Miller, LLP

84 Lumber Company
A. Schulman Inc.
Access Media 3
ACRT, Inc.
Advanced Control
Technologies, Inc.
Advek, Inc.
ADVISA
AES Corporation
Agribusiness Council of
Indiana
Aisin Holdings of
America, Inc.
Akoya, Inc
Akron Thermal
Allison Transmission, Inc.
Altus Capital Partners
American Health Network
American Trim, LLP
American United Life
Insurance Company
Anderson University
Angie's List (ANGI)
AquaCulture Enterprises
Arizona State University
(AZ)
Arlon
Associated General
Contractors of Indiana,
Inc.

Association of Indiana
Counties
Australian Gold, LLP
Auven Therapeutics
Baker-Hill Corporation
Ball State University
Bamar Plastics, Inc.
Baptist Homes of Indiana,
Inc.
Baxter Healthcare
Corporation
BayernLB
BBCN Bank
Beck's Hybrids
Bell Aquaculture
Benedictine University
(IL)
BHI Senior Living, Inc.
Bicycle Garage of Indy,
Inc.
BidPal
Big Lots Stores, Inc.
Big Ten Cancer Research
Consortium Foundation,
Inc.
Black Coaches
Association
Blow Molded Specialties,
Inc.
Bluelock
BMA Management

BNY Mellon
Boathouse Capital
Boise State University
(IA)
Brazosport College
Foundation
Buckingham Companies
Butler University
Cannella Schools of Hair
Design
Capstone Management
Group, LLP
Cardinal Equity Partners
Cardplatforms LLP
Carrier Corporation
Catholic Theological
Union
Celadon Trucking
Services, Inc.
Celtic Capital
Centaur Gaming
Centerfield Capital
Partners, L.P.
Central Indiana
Community Foundation,
Inc.
Central States Rotary
Youth Exchange Program,
Inc.
Centurion Industries, Inc.
CertaPro Painters and
California Closets
CGB Enterprises, Inc.
ChaCha Search, Inc.
Christel House
International
Chrome Deposit
Corporation

Churchill Downs,
Incorporated
CICP Foundation, Inc.
CID Capital
Circle Block Partners,
LLP
Citizens Energy Group
Citizens Resources
City of Indianapolis
City Securities
Corporation
CLAAS
Clabber Girl Corporation
CMA Corporation
Limited
Coastal Partners
Columbus Container, Inc.
Columbus Regional
Hospital
Comlux The Aviation
Group
Community Action of
Greater Indianapolis, Inc
Community Health
Network Foundation
Community Health
Network, Inc.
Community Howard
Regional Health
Community Physicians of
Indiana, Inc.
Compendium
Compuserve Interactive
Services, Inc.
Com-Tech Construction,
Inc.
Conner Prairie
Foundation, Inc.

Conner Prairie Museum, Inc.
Context, P.C.
Cook Group Incorporated
CountryMark Refining and Logistics, LLP
Courseload Inc.
CourseNetworking
Court Holdings Limited
Crown Hill Heritage Foundation
CrownWheel Partners
Culligan International
Culver Educational Foundation, Inc.
Cumberland County College
Cumberland County College Foundation
Cummins, Inc.
Currier Plastics, Inc.
Custom Concrete
D.A. Inc. (Daiwa Kasei Kogyo)
DaimlerChrysler Motors Corporation
Dartmouth College
Deborah Joy Simon Foundation
Deere & Company (John Deere Company)
Dekko Foundation
DePauw University
Development Concepts, Inc.
DFW Capital Partners
Diagnotes
Diemolding Corporation

Digital Audio Disc Corporation (Sony Corporation)
Dinesol Plastics, Inc.
Dominican University (IL)
Dorel Juvenile Group, Inc.
Eastern Illinois University
Eclectic Information
Eleven Fifty Academy, Inc.
Eli Lilly and Company
Emmis Communications
Energy Systems Group LLP
Equian
Escalade, Inc.
ESCAPE Foundation
ESSROC Cement Corporation
Euclid Industries
Everence Association
ExactTarget - Now The Salesforce Marketing Cloud
F.A. Wilhelm Construction Company
Fairfield Manufacturing
Farbest Foods, Inc.
Fifth Third Bank
First Community Bank & Trust
First Farmers Bank and Trust
First Midwest Bank
FirstGroup America
Flat 12 Bierworks
Ford Motor Credit Company

Forest River Foundation, Inc.
Fort Wayne Airport Authority
Franklin County, Ohio
Free Methodist Church of North America
Freudenberg-NOK, G.P.
Frontera Grill
Fuji Component Parts U.S.A., Inc.
Futurex Industries, Inc.
Gary Brackett's IMPACT Foundation, Inc.
Gazelle TechVentures
GE Healthcare
Gene B. Glick Company
Gene B. Glick Family Housing Foundation, Inc.
General Cage LLP
General Electric Capital Corporation
George Washington University
German American Bancorp
GetOutMom.com
Girl Scouts of Hoosier Capital Council, Inc.
Glick Family Foundation
Goshen College
Grace Brethren Investment Foundation, Inc.
Great States Corporation
Greif, Inc. (industrial packaging)
GSI Group LLP
Guide Corporation

H.A. Parts Products of Indiana Company
Halderman Farm Management
Handy & Harman
Hanover College
Harvard University
Haynes International, Inc.
HDG Mansur
Heartland Bancshares, Inc.
Heron Capital
Hilan Capital
Hispania Capital Partners
Hi-Tech Mold and Tool LLP
Hoffman-LaRoche Inc.
Hog Slat Group
Holden America, Inc.
Home Run Realty
Hoosier Cancer Research Network, Inc.
Hoosier Motor Club
Hoosier Park
Hoosiers for Economic Growth, Inc.
Housatonic Community College Foundation, Inc.
Huntington National Bank
Husky Energy
IDI Composites
Illinois College
Illinois Finance Authority
Illinois Public Pension Fund Association (IL)
Illinois Soybean Association
Illinois Soybean Program Operating Board

Illinois State University
ImmuneWorks, Inc.
Indiana Association of
Cities & Towns
Indiana Association of
Homes and Services for
the Aging Inc.
Indiana Association of
United Ways
Indiana Black Expo, Inc.
Indiana Bond Bank
Indiana Chamber of
Commerce
Indiana Corn Growers
Association
Indiana Corn Marketing
Council
Indiana Department of
Transportation
Indiana Family and Social
Services Administration
Indiana Finance Authority
Indiana Health and
Educational Facility
Financing Authority
Indiana Health
Information Technology,
Inc.
Indiana Hemophilia and
Thrombosis Center, Inc.
Indiana Historical Society
Indiana Housing and
Community Development
Authority
Indiana Insolvency, Inc.
Indiana Japanese
Language School, Inc.

Indiana Medical History
Museum
Indiana Municipal Power
Agency
Indiana Packers
Corporation
Indiana Secondary Market
for Education Loans, Inc.
Indiana Stadium and
Convention Building
Authority
Indiana State University
Indiana University
Indiana University Health
Indiana University Purdue
University Indianapolis
Indianapolis Airport
Authority
Indianapolis Foundation,
Inc.
Indianapolis Institute for
Cognitive Therapy
Indianapolis Metropolitan
Professional Firefighters
Union Local 416
Indianapolis Motor
Speedway Corporation
Indianapolis Motor
Speedway Foundation,
Inc.
Indianapolis
Neighborhood Housing
Partnership
Indianapolis Power &
Light
Indianapolis Super Bowl
Legacy Project

Indianapolis Zoological
Society, Inc.
Indy Chamber
Infinity Molding and
Assembly, Inc.
INTAT Precision, Inc.
Integra Bank
Integrated Resources, LLP
Interactive Intelligence,
Inc.
Interior Supply, Inc.
Irving Materials, Inc.
Ivy Tech Community
College of Indiana
Ivy Tech Foundation, Inc.
Jasper Rubber Products,
Inc.
John W. Anderson
Foundation
Johnson & Johnson
JP Morgan Chase Bank,
N.A.
Judd Leighton Foundation
Kansas Board of Regents
(KS)
Kellogg Community
College Foundation
Kirr Marbach & Company
Kite Realty Group Trust
KTC Promotional
Products, Inc.
Lake County Convention
and Visitors Bureau
Lake Land College
Foundation
Lake Superior State
University
Lenex Steel Company

Liaison Technologies, Inc.
Life Spine, LLP
Lineage Capital
Localstake
Lords Seed
Loving Care Agency, Inc.
Lucas Oil Products, Inc.
M.M. Chopra Foundation,
Inc.
Magnequench
International, Inc. a
division of Neo Material
Technologies
Marian University
Marion General Hospital
Marshall University
MASCO Corporation
MB Financial Bank
McCormick Theological
Seminary
McDonald's Corporation
Mechanical Contractors
Association of America,
Inc.
Mechanical Contractors
Association of Chicago
Mechanical Contractors
Association of Iowa
Mechanical Contractors
Association of Northwest
Pennsylvania
Medtronic, Inc.
MedVet Associates, LLP
MET Plastics Inc.
Metro Plastics
Technologies, Inc.
Midwest Ag Finance
Monmouth College (IL)

Monro Muffler Brake, Inc.
Monroe County
Community School
Corporation
Monument Advisors, Inc.
Morgan Foods, Inc.
Morton Arboretum (IL)
Mount Carmel Health
System (OH)
Murray State College
Foundation
MVC Capital
MW Industries, Inc.
My Best Friend's Hair
National Fastpitch
Coaches Association
National FFA Foundation,
Incorporated
National FFA
Organization
National Wine & Spirits,
Inc.
Nationwide Bank
Nevada System of Higher
Education (NV)
Nextech, Inc.
NHK Seating of America,
Inc.
NICO Corporation
North Central Texas
College Foundation
North Park University
Northern Arizona
University
Northwest Nazarene
University
Novartis Pharmaceuticals
Corporation

Nursefinders of
Indianapolis, Inc.
Oak Street Funding
Oakbrook Hotels &
Resorts
Oakland University
ObTech Corp.
Oerlikon Fairfield
OFS Capital Corporation
Old National Bank
One Mission Society, Inc.
OneAmerica
Ontario Corporation
Outokumpu Stainless Pipe
Outokumpu Stainless Plate
Outsourced Administrative
Services, Inc.
Parish Manufacturing
Park Place/RDI Caesars
Park Tudor Foundation,
Inc.
Pedcor Investments
Pension Fund of the
Christian Church
(Disciples of Christ)
Performance Assessment
Network
PERQ
PharmaHub
Phi Kappa Psi Foundation
Pilgrim Lutheran Church
Plainfield-Guilford
Township Public Library
Plastic Components, Inc.
Ports of Indiana
Port-to-Port Consulting
Praesidian Capital
Pratt & Whitney

PRD, Inc.
Procter & Gamble
Company
Purdue University
Quincy University
R&D Molders, Inc.
Randolph Community
College Foundation
Regenstrief Foundation,
Inc.
Regenstrief Institute, Inc.
Reid Hospital and Health
Care Services
Remy Inc.
Remy International
RepuCare
Rhodes State College
Foundation
Richard M. Fairbanks
Foundation, Inc.
Rick L. Stanley Real
Estate, LLP
Ritchie Automation
Robinson-Nugent, Inc.
Rockwell Automation
Rose-Hulman Institute of
Technology
Royer Corporation
Rutgers, The State
University of New Jersey
Sagamore Institute
Saint Bonaventure
University
Saint Mary of the Woods
College
Saint Mary's College
Salin Bank
Samerian Foundation, Inc.

San Diego State
University
San Jacinto College
Foundation
Saturday Evening Post
Society, Inc.
School Choice Indiana
Network, Inc.
Sea-lect Plastics
Corporation
Select Milk Producers,
Inc.
Seton Hall University
Sexton Companies
Shiel Sexton Company,
Inc.
Simon Youth Foundation
Simplex Solutions, Inc.
Simulex, Inc.
Skyline Corporation
SL Liquidating
SonarMed, Inc.
South Atlantic Conference
Soy Aquaculture Alliance
Soy Aquaculture
Association
Sport Graphics
Steak 'n Shake, Inc.
Stenz Corporation
Stewart-MacDonald
Manufacturing Company
Stock Building Supply
Stonehenge Partners
Stoops Freightliner-
Quality Trailer, Inc.
Summa Health System
SYDA Foundation

Symbios Medical
Products, LLP
Talbert Manufacturing
Talbert Manufacturing
Co., Inc.
Target Corporation
Taylor University
Teays River Investments,
LLP
Tech Molded Plastics L.P.
Technicolor
TeenWorks
Terra College Foundation
The Buckingham
Companies
The Center for Food
Integrity
The Children's Museum of
Indianapolis
The Coca-Cola Company
The Friedman Foundation
for Educational Choice
The Gettys Group, Inc.
The Heritage Group
The Keller Manufacturing
Co., Inc.
The Lafayette Life
Insurance Company
The Mind Trust, Inc.
The Northern Trust
Company
The OneAmerica
Foundation, Inc.
The Orchard School
The Order of United
Commercial Travelers of
America (OH)
The Policy Circle, Co.

The Sycamore Institute,
Inc.
Think Forward
Foundation, Inc.
Thogus Products
Company
Time Compression
TinderBox
Tipton County
Foundation, Inc.
Tomy Corporation
Trademark Plastics, Inc.
Trupointe Cooperative,
Inc.
TTE Technology, Inc.
Tulsa Community College
Tulsa Community College
Foundation
Universal Music Group
University High School of
Indiana, Inc.
University of Alabama
University of California,
Los Angeles
University of Cincinnati
University of Dayton
University of Evansville
University of Georgia
Research Foundation
University of Illinois
University of Notre Dame
University of Oklahoma
University of Southern
California
University of Southern
Indiana
University of the Virgin
Islands

US Bank
Vectren Corporation
Verallia Saint-Gobain
Containers
Vertellus Specialties Inc.
Veterinary Study Groups,
Inc.
Viking Plastics
Villa St. Benedict
Village of Lombard,
Illinois
Vincennes University
VIP Tooling, Inc.
Vistex
Vistex Foundation (IL)
Vontoo, Inc.
Wabash College
Wabash Valley
Broadcasting Corporation
Walker Information, Inc.
Wal-Mart Stores, Inc.

Walther Cancer
Foundation, Inc.
Walther Cancer Institute
Wausau Insurance
Companies
Weatherford College
West Virginia University
WFYI
Whalaa, Inc.
Wheaton College
White Energy
White Wolf Capital
William L. West
Wine and Spirits
Wholesalers of Indiana
Wintrust Banks
Wisconsin Lutheran
College
Wisdom Tools, Inc.
Wyndham Hotels and
Resorts

Appendix B

Foundational E-email Series
Sent by and to
The Author – Lee B. Baker

From: leebbaker@hotmail.com
To: Media Outlets and Indiana State Senators
Subject: Ice Miller Law Firm coerces Deputy Chief of Indianapolis Police
Date: Sun, 13 Sep 2015 04:04:42 -0600

Ice Miller Law Firm Coerces Deputy Chief of Indianapolis Police Department

Apparently the Deputy Chief of the Indianapolis Metropolitan Police Department, Bryan K. Roach was coerced on the afternoon of 31 July 2015, by a Senior Partner of the Indianapolis Law Firm of Ice Miller, to frustrate the proper execution of a Court Order issued by the Honorable Patrick Dietrick, Criminal Division Judge.

According to information from the Hamilton County Sheriff, Mark J. Bowen, Deputy Chief Roach of IMPD requested Deputy Chris Yates and Deputy Jason Cramer to unlawfully "add" non-Court Documents to a packet of Official Documents from the Marion Superior Court, Criminal Division under the authority of Indiana Code 34-26-5-9.

The probable motivation to risk such a daring action by the Deputy Chief of Police was simple Religious retribution. Within the "Priesthood" power-structure of The Church of Jesus Christ of Latter-day Saints (Mormons) the Area Authority for the State of Indianapolis is a Mr. Paul H.

Sinclair, who by chance is a Senior Partner of Ice Miller, who by chance is the Spiritual Leader of Deputy Chief Roach, who by chance holds a much lower "Priesthood" rank, than of Mr. Sinclair.

It should be noted that at times, the secret ceremonies and rituals of "Priesthood Loyalty" conducted within the Mormon Temples, have been required at the risk of taking one's own life by slicing the throat from ear to ear.

As if the Deputies of Hamilton County and the Documents of the Marion Superior Court were both the personal tools of Ice Miller and The Mormon Church, it is apparent that Mr. Sinclair instructed the Indianapolis Deputy Chief of Police to add a few documents to the Court's Official packet. Not surprisingly the documents to be added were from Ice Miller and The Mormon Church, apparently to give some authority or association between these two very deceptive organizations and the Marion Superior Court.

What should be alarming to the Public is that the power, authority and control of the Mormon "Priesthood" have been actively employed countless times to impede and frustrate both Local and National laws for many, many years.

As a Former Mormon Bishop who has participated in all of these secret "Priesthood Loyalty" ceremonies, I now question, who... who... can a visitor to Indiana trust?

It is common knowledge that the State of Utah has many issues of religious and legal conflicts of interest. Now that the City of Carmel, just north of Indianapolis, has accepted the newest Mormon Temple, will the Police, Courts and Rule of Law in Indiana now follow the example of Utah?

Sincerely,

Lee B. Baker

From: Mark.Bowen@hamiltoncounty.in.gov
To: leebbaker@hotmail.com
Subject: RE: Hamilton County - Documents for Pre-Trial
Date: Thu, 3 Sep 2015 14:16:52 +0000

Mr. Baker,

The answers to your questions are highlighted in **BOLD** and follow the questions in the e-mail correspondence below.

Respectfully,

Mark J. Bowen

Mark J. Bowen, Sheriff
Hamilton County Sheriff's Office
18100 Cumberland Rd.
Noblesville, IN 46060
(317) 773-1872

From: Lee Baker [mailto:leebbaker@hotmail.com]
Sent: Wednesday, September 02, 2015 11:11 AM
To: Mark J. Bowen
Cc: confidential@atg.in.gov
Subject: Hamilton County - Documents for Pre-Trial

Sheriff Bowen,

As I prepare for a public Hearing / Trial on this matter, at this time, I would formally ask your Office to provide the following information:

1. The names of the Deputies who wrongfully added the Ice Miller and Mormon Church documents to the Official Court Packet to be served.

Deputy Chris Yates and Deputy Jason Cramer.

2. The name of the individual(s) who represented Ice Miller and/or the Mormon Church, when these documents were provided to the Deputies and then added to the Official Court Packet to be served.

Brian Roach

3. The location (building) in which the Ice Miller and Mormon Church documents were provided to the Deputies.

The parking lot of the church located at 116th and Springmill Road.

4. Any relevant instructions, guidance, requests or demands given to the Deputies by the representative(s) of Ice Miller and the Mormon Church.

Deputy Yates was asked to deliver the documents.

5. Any unique or specific instructions provided by the Court that may have altered the understanding or actions of the Deputies.

None

Thank you in advance for your support.   *Lee B. Baker*

From: Mark.Bowen@hamiltoncounty.in.gov
To: leebbaker@hotmail.com
Subject: RE: Formal Question of Ethics for Hamilton County
Date: Mon, 24 Aug 2015 13:56:47 +0000

Mr. Baker,

I received your inquiry regarding the propriety of a Deputy delivering
other documents (those not issued by a court) when serving official court
documents. It is not normal practice for this to occur. The Deputy
involved has been counseled to serve (deliver) only those documents
issued by the court, when called upon to do so.

Respectfully,

Mark J. Bowen

Mark J. Bowen, Sheriff
Hamilton County Sheriff's Office
18100 Cumberland Rd.
Noblesville, IN 46060
(317) 773-1872

From: Lee Baker [mailto:leebbaker@hotmail.com]
Sent: Thursday, August 20, 2015 8:42 PM
To: WA Farley; Mark J. Bowen
Cc: steven.humke@icemiller.com; Lee Baker
Subject: Formal Question of Ethics for Hamilton County

Would the Leadership of Hamilton County please tell me why it's Officers
were acting as a delivery service for The Mormon Church and the Law Firm of
Ice Miller?

Thank you,

Respectfully,

Lee B Baker

From: ima@indygov.org
To: leebbaker@hotmail.com
Subject: Re: Contact the Mayor online
Date: Thu, 20 Aug 2015 13:02:57 -0400

Good afternoon, Mr. Baker:

On behalf of the Mayor's Office, I have received your message concerning procedures with law enforcement officers delivering personal correspondence. Upon checking the return of service computer entry, it was Hamilton County law officials that served the protective order to you and I assume the other letter.   To inquire about their procedures, please contact them at 317-776-9600 or at http://www.hamiltoncounty.in.gov/Directory.aspx?did=54 (copy and paste into browser).

Thank you,

Judy Flannery

Constituent Services Assistant
Office of Mayor Greg Ballard – City of Indianapolis

www.indy.gov - Newsletter - Facebook - Twitter - Flikr

A Question of Ethics within Hamilton County Government

RE: Case number 49G21-1507-PO-024527, July 31 2015: Marion Superior Court 21, Criminal Division (49G21), State of Indiana, Myla A. Eldridge, Clerk of the Court.

On the afternoon of Wednesday the 5th of August, I was served with a Court Order of Protection specific to Mr. Paul H. Sinclair (Partner of Ice Miller, Law Firm and a Senior Representative of The Church of Jesus Christ of Latter-day Saints, a.k.a. The Mormons)

As representatives of the Court and the State of Indiana, the Order was served by two uniformed Officers (State Patrol or County Sheriff). Upon exiting the new multi-million dollar Mormon Temple, embossed with the statement: "**Holiness to the Lord**" these Officers of the Law served me with private and personal letters from both the Law Offices of Ice Miller and The

Headquarters of The Church of Jesus Christ of Latter-day Saints, a.k.a. The Mormons.

Both letters communicated the intent to take civil and criminal action if I were to continue what they both considered "harassment, stalking, threatening, violent, sex offense, annoying, or contacting, directly or indirectly" the person of Mr. Sinclair or his family.

It is a matter of public record that all my past communications with and to Mr. Sinclair has been focused on one subject alone, without deviation or variation: *"As a Representative of the Mormon Church and as a Partner of Ice Miller, may I ask you several specific questions as to the practice of your Faith and of your Profession here in the State of Indiana?"*

My questions to the State of Indiana and to the County of Marion, prior to a request for a formal investigation are these:

"Is it customary or legal to employ on-Duty Officers of the Law as armed couriers of Private Organizations with the expressed intention of communicating or delivering letters, which although relative to the subject, are not the official communications of either the State or the County?"

"If this service is both authorized and approved by the State or County, would this then open to the Public the opportunity to include with any officially delivered Court Order (Eviction, Divorce, Restraint, etc.) a private or personal letter from a third-party not represented by or for the State or County. Could this tax paid service then include additional letters of instructions, desires, demands or affection?"

I enthusiastically await your response to these questions.

Sincerely,

Lee B. Baker

The Offices of Ice Miller and the Mormon Church – A Corrupt and Racist Combination

Open Letter to Religious and Business Organization or Clients and Regulatory Agencies

August 2015

The following information is provided as a warning to both the Worldwide Religious and Business Communities as well as to the General Public. This personal analysis and commentary has been developed from the perspective and background of a Senior Intelligence Officer for the United States Government with special training and access as an International Counter-terrorism Instructor with 36 years of service with The National Security Agency and the Central Intelligence Agencies, Washington, D.C. Furthermore, as a former Senior Leader of The Church of Jesus Christ of Latter-day Saints, (Bishop, High Priest, Instructor and Temple Historian), the Mormon Church information presented here is both precise and official.

The purpose of this article is to provide a graphic link between the deceptive business practices of the *Ice Miller LLP*, legal counsel (icemiller.com) and the deceitful religious doctrine of the *Mormon Church* (lds.org). The disturbing shared component between these two dishonest organizations is a Mr. Paul H. Sinclair, who is a respected Senior Partner at Ice Miller, LLP. (One American Square, Suite 2900, Indianapolis, IN 46282-0200), and a very Senior Leader (Elder or General Authority) of The Church of Jesus Christ of Latter-day Saints (Mormons), Salt Lake City, UT.

On the afternoon of the 17th of July 2015, I greeted Mr. Sinclair from the Law Firm of Ice Miller with a warm handshake on the south steps of the new Mormon Temple, Carmel, IN., which cost an estimated 52 million dollars. I had prepared a few questions about how Women, Homosexuals and Blacks have been treated within the Mormon Church and I was seeking his personal opinion of the oversight of the Government of the United States of

America. He asked me to wait "right here" on the steps, then he disappeared into a Church annex building, never to return.

He must have known that women have been shared and traded like cattle among the Leadership of the Mormon Church and that Homosexuals and Blacks have long been viewed with distain and derision as a matter of policy, doctrine and practice. As an Intelligence Officer with more than three decades of service to the United States and its foreign business Partners, I have found the long history of dishonesty and anti-American practices of the Mormon Church most disturbing.

"God says "Go and obey my law." Congress says "No, you shall not do it." Now the question is-who shall we obey?" – *Formal Warning from a Mormon Prophet*

Without question the Leadership of the Mormon Church knows well the very anti-American teachings of its founding Prophet Joseph Smith Jr. and the 80 years of a secret[1] **"Oath of Vengeance"** against the United States of American within the Mormon Temples like the one built just north of Indianapolis. Specifically, that Oath taken by the Mormons, under the penalty of Death was: *"You and each of you do covenant and promise that you will pray and never cease to pray to Almighty God to avenge the blood of the prophets "upon this nation", and that you will teach the same to your children and to your children's children unto the third and fourth generations"* The Mormon Prophet Joseph Smith Jr. even openly compared himself to Mohammad and referenced the Quran of Islam. As a comparison to the Book of Mormon, an Official Mormon periodical claims: *"No other book, since the Quran, has given birth to a People."* In yet another formal statement from the Mormon Church they state: *"It is now known that the Quran, the only book claiming an equal amount of divine inspiration and accuracy..."* What the current Mormon Church now projects as a very patriotic foundation is extremely shallow and very deceptive.

It is ominous that the American Law Firm of Ice Miller not only supports but actively defends both the formal Doctrine of the

Mormon Faith and promotes its Leadership who has been formally instructed in discriminatory, sexists and homophobic teachings.

I have no doubt that the average member of the Mormon Faith may be both Patriotic and believe them to be Christian. This is only possible if they are intentionally ignorant of the Formal and Official History, Doctrine and Teachings of The Church of Jesus Christ of Latter-day Saints. The Mormon Church has, for most of its history been so anti-American and violently opposed to the Rule of Law that the United States Senate, the United States Congress and a number of Presidents have considered them so radical and extreme that they have publically warned the American People as to the Mormon immoral practices and secret ceremonies.

My wife, three daughters and three granddaughters have found it offensive beyond description that the "Prophet" of Mormonism, Joseph Smith Jr. had taken two 14 year-old girls as wives when he was 37. Even more repulsive is the fact that Smith took the wives of at least a dozen other men to share among the Church Leadership. Church records indicate that he took a Mother and Daughter and four sets of Sisters as potential sexual partners.

According to the formal Doctrine of the Mormon Church, **no** Black African or any man or women with a single drop of Black African blood, was **ever** worthy, righteous or moral enough throughout the total History of Humanity to be saved... until this current generation.

Within the Current, yes the Current Doctrine and Scriptures [2] of the Mormon Faith, it is taught as a matter of fact that **Black** skin on a human was a reflection of a curse from God. Additionally, it is taught today that if a human became more righteous and honorable, then their skin would turn **White**. Following are only a few of the hundreds of examples of such teaching from the Mormon Faith:

"Nigger, Darky, Sambo, Black Representative of the Devil with the Curse from God of a Skin of Blackness"

Considered Mormon Scripture – These several terms have been used liberally to describe the African American Race by many Mormon Prophets, Apostles and Leaders within the Mormon Scriptures and Official General Conferences of the Mormon Church as well as in various Official Mormon Publications.

"And after the flood we are told that the curse [skin of blackness] that had been pronounced upon Cain was continued through Ham's wife, as he had married a wife of that seed. And why did it pass through the flood? Because it was necessary that the Devil should have a representation upon the earth as well as God". – *Official Scripture by the Mormon Church Prophet*

"Why are so many of the inhabitants of the earth cursed with a Skin of Blackness? It comes in consequence of their fathers rejecting the power of the Holy Priesthood and the law of God. They will go down to death." – *Official Scripture by the Mormon Church Prophet*

"Even if we treat our slaves in an oppressive manner, it is still none of their business and they [United States Government] ought not to meddle with it." – *Official Scripture by the Mormon Church Prophet*

"There never has been a plural marriage by the consent or sanction or knowledge or approval of the church since the manifesto" – *Official Statement by the Mormon Church Prophet recording the Congressionally documented lie of the Mormon Prophet Joseph F. Smith to the U.S. Senate, Committee on Privileges and Elections.*

"On 1 February, preaches his [Mormon Prophet John Taylor] last public sermon and, in hopes of limiting the persecution against the Church by Federal authorities, goes into hiding." – *Official Scripture by the Mormon Church Prophet*

I do not submit these horrible and disgusting matters to the Religious and Business Communities in an effort to unreasonably degrade or damage the character or reputation of Mr. Paul H. Sinclair, as I believe him to be a perfect representative of both Ice Mille, LLP. and the Mormon Church. My position and opinion is this: that after my 36-years of specifically dealing with the clandestine operations of known or suspected radical or extremist Organizations, I am genuinely concerned with Mr. Sinclair's ability to function as an honest representative of the Law, International Trade or with even the least degree of integrity regarding his moral standards.

Without question, the well documented patterns of historically recurring counterculture training and subversive activities of such Organizations are not entirely unlike the essential loyalties and secret pledges (to the point of death) taken by the elite membership of The Church of Jesus Christ of Latter-day Saints.

I do stand firm in my assessment and analysis that if required, Mr. Paul H. Sinclair as a High Priest after the Order of Melchizedek in the Mormon Faith would not hesitate for a moment to follow the direction of the Prophet of the Mormon Church without regard to the legal, moral or ethical nature of his actions. As an Officer and Representative of the Law, I seriously believe that Mr. Paul H. Sinclair's loyalties require a higher standard of scrutiny than normally associated with the general public when serving in the business community at large.

Regrettably a small slice of Utah has come to central Indiana simply because the local Christian Community has been both misinformed and uninformed specific to the true Doctrine of the Mormon Church. Yes, the dominant Church of Utah has been welcomed by the City of Carmel and the State of Indiana, probably without the knowledge that they bring with them the Nation's highest rate of teen suicide, adult addition to anti-depressants and on-line pornography in addition to their secret handshakes, signs, tokens and passwords.

Even more disturbing is the fact that within the State of Indiana the Honorable Judge Patrick Dietrick and the Marion County Clerk, Myla A. Eldridge (a professional African American woman who, most likely, has never read The Book of Mormon[3]), have ruled that the above true and well documented information alone, when communicated to you, is somehow "A Threat of Violence, Harassing, Annoying, Sexually Offensive or a form of Stalking of the family of Mr. Sinclair" and thus worthy of an Order of Protection for a Member of the Indiana Bar Association. How embarrassing for Marion County and the State of Indiana. How can the Truth about Mormonism be offensive to anyone... but a Mormon?

Most Sincerely,

Lee B. Baker

United States Army Officer (Ret.)
Disabled Veteran (Legion of Merit Recipient)
Counter-terrorism Instructor, National Security Agency (Ret.)
Former Mormon High Priest and Ordained Bishop (Ashamed)

Legal Notice: This personal commentary has been developed and issued under an Ex Parte Order for Protection from the Marion County, Indiana, Superior Court, Criminal Division, Case Number 49G21-1507-PO-024527, as such this information is for **you** (the recipient) and is not intended (directly or indirectly) for the Petitioner (Mr. Paul H. Sinclair). The above subjective information is "**About**" Mr. Sinclair, Partner of the Law Offices of Ice Miller and a Senior Leader within the Mormon Church and is not "**To**" Mr. Sinclair, as such you instructed not to share this information "**With**" Mr. Sinclair.

[1] *Mormon Scripture – Temple Oath of Vengeance, U.S. Senate Document 486 (59th Congress, 1st Session) Proceedings Before the Committee on Privileges and Elections of the United States Senate in the Matter of the Protests Against the Right of Hon. Reed Smoot, a Senator from the State of Utah, to hold his Seat.* 4 vols. [+1 vol. index] (Washington: Library of Congress - Government Printing Office, 1906

[2] 1 Nephi 11:13, 1 Nephi 12:23, 1 Nephi 13:15, 2 Nephi 5:21, 2 Nephi 30:6, Jacob 3:5, Jacob 3:8-9, Alma 3:6, Alma 3:9, Alma 3:14, Alma 23:18, 3 Nephi 2:14-16, 3 Nephi 19:25, 30, Mormon 5:15, Moses 7:8, Moses 7:12, Moses 7:22, Abraham 1:21, Abraham 1:27

[3] 1 Nephi 11:13, 1 Nephi 12:23, 1 Nephi 13:15, 2 Nephi 5:21, 2 Nephi 30:6, Jacob 3:5, Jacob 3:8-9, Alma 3:6, Alma 3:9, Alma 3:14, Alma 23:18, 3 Nephi 2:14-16, 3 Nephi 19:25, 30, Mormon 5:15

Appendix C

Initial Plea Agreement – State of Indiana

STATE OF INDIANA

IN THE MARION COUNTY
SUPERIOR COURT

CRIMINAL DIVISION ROOM 3
COUNTY OF MARION

STATE OF INDIANA

v.

CAUSE NO.
49G031509F5033343

Lee Baker

PLEA AGREEMENT

The Defendant, in person and by counsel, and the State of Indiana, hereby enters into this plea agreement made pursuant to negotiations. The parties agree as follows:

1. This agreement, signed by the Defendant, Defense Counsel, and the Deputy Prosecuting Attorney assigned to the above case, shall be introduced into evidence by stipulation of all the parties at the time of the guilty plea.

2. Defendant enters into this agreement knowing that the Court has the authority to accept or reject the agreement and understands that the Court may take the Defendant's criminal record into consideration in determining whether to accept or reject this plea agreement.

3. The Defendant agrees to plead guilty to: **Count IV, Invasion of Privacy, a class A misdemeanor, Count V, Invasion of Privacy, a class A misdemeanor, and Count VI, Invasion of Privacy, a class A misdemeanor. The State will dismiss all remaining counts.**

4.   At the time of the taking of the guilty plea and again at the time of the Defendant's sentencing, the State reserves the right to question witnesses and comment on any evidence presented on which the Court may rely to determine the sentence to be imposed; to present testimony or statements from the victim(s) or victim representative(s), and the State of Indiana and the Defendant agrees that the Court shall impose the following sentence: **The total sentence shall be 3 years with an agreement that all of that time be suspended and 3 years on probation. The probation shall be non-reporting. As a specific condition of probation the defendant shall have no contact, direct or indirect, with Paul Sinclair. Indirect contact shall include having another individual attempt to contact Mr. Sinclair in any way. Additionally, the no contact order shall mean that the defendant and/or any other individual acting at his direction shall have no contact of any kind with Paul Sinclair's family members, Paul Sinclair's church, and Paul Sinclair's employer and/or clients of his employer. Contact, direct or indirect, shall include, but not be limited to; in-person contact, telephone calls, text messages, e-mails, literature, and mailings.**

5.   Defendant hereby waives the right to appeal any sentence imposed by the Court, including the right to seek appellate review of the sentence pursuant to Indiana Appellate Rule 7(B), so long as the Court sentences the defendant within the terms of this plea agreement (   ).

6.   The Defendant acknowledges that the State's recommendation, or agreement to make no recommendation, is based on the Defendant's criminal history known to the Deputy Prosecutor representing the State at the time this agreement is executed and who entered into the agreement. If this information is incomplete, or that a further or more accurate criminal history is discovered prior to the entry of judgment, or the Defendant is charged with the commission of another offense prior to sentencing, the State reserves the right to unilaterally withdraw from this agreement at any time prior to the entry of judgment herein.(   ).

7.   The Defendant understands and acknowledges by his/her initials that if this agreement is accepted by the Court the Defendant will give up the following rights:

        _____ (a)   the right to a public and speedy trial by jury;

_____ (b) the right to confront and cross examine the witnesses against him/her;

_____ (c) the right to have compulsory process for obtaining witnesses in his/her favor;

_____ (d) the right to require the State to prove his/her guilt beyond a reasonable doubt;

_____ (e) the right to remain silent and the right not to be compelled to testify against oneself;

_____ (f) the right to present evidence on one's own behalf and to be presumed innocent until proven guilty beyond a reasonable doubt.

8. The Defendant further acknowledges that entry of a guilty plea pursuant to this agreement constitutes an admission of the truth of all facts alleged in the charge or counts to which the Defendant pleads guilty and that entry of the guilty plea will result in a conviction on those charges or counts. ( ). The Defendant also understands that by pleading guilty he/she gives up the right to appeal the conviction ( ).

9. The Defendant acknowledges satisfaction with Defense Counsel's representation and competency in this matter ( ). The Defendant believes this agreement to be in the Defendant's best interest ( ).

10. The Defendant acknowledges that he/she has a right to pursue post-conviction relief, if there is a legal and factual basis to do so, and that entering a guilty plea herein does not operate as a waiver of that right. ( ).

11. The Defendant acknowledges that if he/she is not a natural born United States Citizen, signing this plea agreement could affect immigration status. Defendant has discussed fully with his / her counsel the effect of signing this agreement on his/her citizenship status. ( ).

12. The Defendant understands and acknowledges his awareness that admission to Invasion of Privacy in this instance may have collateral consequences should he be charged for the same or a

similar offense in the future; collateral consequences may include charging and/or sentence enhancement (_____).

13. This agreement embodies the entire agreement between the parties and no promises or inducements have been made or given to the Defendant by the State which is not part of this written agreement. (   ).

14. Pursuant to Administrative Rule 9(G) (6)(a) and I.C. 35-33-3-3, the Defendant and the State waive the right to exclude the pending plea agreement from Public Access. (   ).

_____

Defendant

_____

Defendant's Counsel

_____

Deputy Prosecutor

I certify that I have informed the victim and / or victim's representative of the fact that the State has entered into discussions with defense counsel concerning this agreement and of the contents of the State's recommendation, if any; and, that I will notify the victim and his/her representative of the opportunity to be present when the Court considers the recommendation.

_____

Deputy Prosecutor

Appendix D

Racist Doctrine from the 2016 version of the Book of Mormon

1 Nephi 12:23 (prophecy of the Lamanites) " became a *dark,* and *loathsome,* and a *filthy people,* full of idleness and all manner of abominations."

1 Nephi 13:15 (Gentiles) "they were *white, and exceedingly fair and beautiful,* like unto my people [Nephites] before they were slain."

2 Nephi 5:21 "a sore cursing . . . *as they were white,* and exceedingly fair and delightsome, that they might not be enticing unto my people the *Lord God did cause a skin of blackness* to come upon them."

2 Nephi 30:6 (prophecy to the Lamanites if they repented) "scales of darkness shall begin to fall. . . . they shall be a *white and delightsome* people" ("white and delightsome" was changed to *"pure and delightsome"* in 1981).

Jacob 3:5 (Lamanites cursed) "whom ye hate because of *their filthiness* and the cursing which hath come upon their skins"

Jacob 3:8-9 "their skins will be *whiter* than yours... revile no more against them because of the darkness of their skins. . . ."

Alma 3:6 "And the skins of the *Lamanites were dark,* according to the mark which was set upon their fathers, *which was a curse* upon them because of their *transgression and their rebellion."*

Alma 3:9 "whosoever did mingle his seed with that of the Lamanites did bring the same *curse* upon his seed."

Alma 3:14 (Lamanites cursed) "set a mark on them that they and their seed may be separated from thee and thy seed. . . ."

3 Nephi 2:14-16 "Lamanites who had united with the Nephites were numbered among the Nephites; And their curse was taken from them, and *their skin became white like unto the Nephites* and . . . became exceedingly fair. . . . "

3 Nephi 19:25, 30 (Disciples) "they were as *white* as the countenance and also the garments of Jesus; and behold the *whiteness* thereof did exceed all the *whiteness*. . . . nothing upon earth so white as the *whiteness* thereof... and behold they *were white, even as Jesus."*

Appendix E

Three Basic Questions for Elder Paul H. Sinclair

Question One

As recorded within the History of the Church, Volume 2, Chapter 18, page 247 (see link below), as also within the Joseph Smith Jr. Papers (on lds.org) and the Official 1835 to 1876 version of the Doctrine and Covenants Section 101, Verse 4, (see link below), the Mormon Church clearly and boldly stated that they did **not** support, sanction or practice Polygamy. The specific authorized Mormon Church statement in question is:

"In asmuch as this church of Christ has been reproached with the crime of fornication, and polygamy: we declare that we believe, that one man should have one wife; and one woman, but one husband, except in case of death, when either is at liberty to marry again."

See: http://josephsmithpapers.org/paperSummary/statement-on-marriage-17-august-1835?

This false and very deceptive "Scripture" was used on many occasions by Elder John Taylor and others (according to his own journals) during his Mission in England to convert hundreds under the promise that the Church did **not** practice Polygamy, when in fact it did and he, himself, when making these statements had at least eight wives of his own. This was certainly no printing error or publisher's mistake, this was a supposed valid Mormon Doctrine freely given, multiple times to the Officers and Representatives of the United States Government, the various Magistrates of the Local and State Courts.

Additionally, this statement of obvious deception was instrumental in the conversion of hundreds of unsuspecting investigators of the Mormon Faith, but it was actually a bold lie. How does this well documented and hideous lie of the Mormon

Church fall within any standard of respectable Christian behavior or moral respect to those seeking the True will of God or in any way, a reflection of the core teachings of Jesus Christ?

http://josephsmithpapers.org/paperSummary/statement-on-marriage-17-august-1835?

and

https://www.lds.org/topics/plural-marriage-in-kirtland-and-nauvoo?lang=eng

Question Two

Joseph Smith Jr. (1805-1844) claimed to be a Prophet of God. The Mormon Church declares that as an authorized Prophet of God, he, Joseph Smith Jr. accurately corrected thousands of errors in the Bible. If this one correction in The Old Testament, the Book of Genesis, Chapter 17, Verse 11, is precise according to Joseph Smith Jr. and the Mormon Church, then it means that the Covenant of Circumcision from God was misunderstood by Abraham, or then incorrectly written by Moses and then it was done absolutely improperly for over 3,000 years by Every Prophet of God, and every Jewish Male that has ever lived, to include **Jesus Christ Himself**.

This critical mistake to the first and most significant of all Covenants between God and the Nation and Kingdom of Israel was, in the Mormon view; apparently done under the watchful eye of God Himself, who then chose to wait until 1834 to spiritually reveal to Joseph Smith Jr. the true and correct procedures of this, His First Covenant with His Chosen People, when it would have absolutely no consequence whatsoever and utterly no effect on any human being.

Or Joseph Smith Jr. in 1843 really did lie about his ability to correct the Bible.

English Grammatical Note for Question Two

Provided here are examples of several other Joseph Smith Jr. Translations and his appropriate and logical use of a semicolon (;) with the phrase: "**that thou mayest know**" as in Genesis, Chapter 17, Verse 11.

These examples are shown to clarify the directly associated subject of two independent statements as used by Joseph Smith Jr. himself and then approved, published and canonized under a copyright of The Church of Jesus Christ of Latter-day Saints, Salt Lake City, Utah.

"On occasion, a writer may decide that the next sentence is so closely connected to the previous one that a slight break is more appropriate than a new sentence. A semicolon can be used for this purpose. Also see the use of a semicolon within a Compound Sentence." Merriam-Webster's Guide to Punctuation and Style, 2001

This information is provided for those who may consider this, the Joseph Smith Jr. Translation to be somehow associated with the Ordinance of Baptism, as so noted within the LDS Footnotes and LDS Bible Dictionary.

This consideration is both absurd and unacceptable as we know that Joseph Smith Jr. had both the knowledge of English and the absolute ability as a "Prophet of God" to use the word "**Baptism**" within this imaginary correction and/or remove the word "**Circumcision**" if he so desired to at any time and in any way. He did not, and the Mormon Church, Editors, Printers and the First Presidency of the Church have accepted this version of Joseph Smith Jr.'s correction for well over 150 years.

It should be noted that no change to Joseph Smith Jr.'s "Translation" of Genesis, Chapter 17, Verse 11 has ever been offered within any of the many successive printing, reprinting and editing of their own copyrighted Mormon Scriptures. As such, I will only consider changes to this Inspired Translation by the Current

Prophet of The Church of Jesus Christ of Latter-day Saints, **all** others, myself included, must deal with it exactly as Joseph Smith Jr. himself has approved it.

- **Ex 8:10**: "And he said, Tomorrow. And he said, Be it according to thy word; **that thou mayest know** that there is none like unto the Lord our God."

- **Ex 9:14:** "For I will at this time send all my plagues upon thine heart, and upon thy servants, and upon thy people; **that thou mayest know** that there is none like me in all the earth."

- **Ex 9:29**: "And Moses said unto him, As soon as I am gone out of the city, I will spread abroad my hands unto the Lord; and the thunder shall cease, neither shall there be any more hail; **that thou mayest know** how that the earth is the Lord's."

- **Ex 10:2**: "And that thou mayest tell in the ears of thy son, and of thy son's son, what things I have wrought in Egypt, and my signs which I have done among them; **that ye may know** how that I am the Lord."

Question Three

The Book of Mormon, as the "Keystone" of the Mormon religion, contains very little in terms of how "Mormonism" is actually taught and practiced by the Mormon Church today. Why is it that the Book of Mormon **does not say anything** about the current and foundational Mormon Practices, Beliefs or Doctrine? How can this statement in the Book of Mormon, about the Book of Mormon be true: "*The Book of Mormon is a volume of holy scripture comparable to the Bible. It is a record of God's dealings with ancient inhabitants of the Americas and contains **the fulness of the everlasting gospel**.*"

How can the Book of Mormon be "the fulness of the everlasting gospel" if so many core Doctrines were added to the

"**Restored Gospel**" that were not recorded or practiced within the Book of Mormon? The central question is this, what would Mormonism really look like today, with just the teachings of the Book of Mormon or is it (the Book of Mormon) not honestly or functionally the "fulness of the everlasting gospel."?

The Exclusive Doctrines of the Mormon Church

None of these Key Doctrines of Mormonism are found in the **Book of Mormon**.

Baptism for the Dead, Celestial or Eternal Marriage or Eternal Families, God was once a Man, Man can become a God, There are many Gods, God has a body of Flesh and Bones, The Father and the Son are Separate Beings, Terrestrial Kingdom – Telestial Kingdom – Celestial Kingdom, Polygamy is of God, Polyandry is of God, Lying is of God, Premortal Life or Pre-Existence with God, Heavenly Mother, Temple Covenants for the Living or the Dead.

The Exclusive Organization of the Mormon Church

None of these Key Elements of Mormonism are found in the **Book of Mormon**.

Name of the Church "Church of Christ", Melchizedek Priesthood, Aaronic Priesthood, Church President, Stake President, Mission President, Temple President, Area Authorities, General Authorities, Bishop, Elders Quorum President, Priest's Quorums, Ward Mission Leader, Relief Society Organization, Branch, Ward, Stakes, Home or Visiting Teaching, Primary, Young Men's and Young Women's Organizations, Fast Offering, or Tithing Settlement.

In view of the above list, how can the Book of Mormon be considered "**the fulness of the everlasting gospel**". In point-of-fact, the Book of Mormon clearly teaches against many of the essential Doctrines of the Mormon Church:

- Instead of teaching that there are many gods, the Book of Mormon teaches that there is only **one** God: (**Mosiah 15:1-5; Alma 11:28;29; 2 Nephi 31:21**)

- Instead of teaching that people evolve or progress to godhood, the Book of Mormon teaches that God is **unchanging**: (**Mormon 9:9,19; Moroni 8:18; Alma 41:8; 3 Nephi 24:6**)

- Instead of teaching that God is a physical, exalted man, the Book of Mormon teaches that God is a **spirit**: (**Alma 18:24-28; 22:9-11**)

- Both Joseph Smith Jr. and Brigham Young taught polygamy, despite the fact that the Book of Mormon **condemned** the practice: (**Jacob 1:15; 2:23,24,27,31; 3:5; Mosiah 11:2,4; Ether 10:5,7**)

Made in the USA
San Bernardino, CA
29 March 2016